## Student Workbook

# CONTEMPORARY
# Living

**Verdene Ryder**
Family Life Education Consultant
Houston, Texas

**Marjorie B. Harter, Ph.D.**
Family Life Education Consultant
Washington, DC

Publisher
**The Goodheart-Willcox Company, Inc.**
Tinley Park, Illinois

# Introduction

This *Student Workbook* is designed for use with the text *Contemporary Living*. It helps you explore many of the concepts introduced in the text more thoroughly. As you complete the activities, you will be asked to examine your thoughts and feelings about yourself, other people, and our society. You will have many opportunities to compare your ideas with those of your classmates.

The activities in this guide are divided into chapters that correspond to the chapters in the text. Some of the activities have "right" answers. However, many of the activities are designed to stimulate you to think, evaluate various situations, and draw your own conclusions. Do not hesitate to express your true feelings and opinions. Activities that ask for your opinions cannot be scored on a "right" or "wrong" basis. On the other hand, you should not complete the activities carelessly. It is to your advantage to give thoughtful consideration to each response you make. The more thought you put into the activities, the more knowledge you will gain from them.

# Table of Contents

## Factors That Shape Your Personality

**Activity A**

**Chapter 1**

Name _____

Date _____ Period _____

Imagine you are a Web page designer. In the space below, design a Web page that reflects your personality. You can use words, drawings, or glue photos in the space provided. On the following page, analyze your Web site and answer questions that describe your personality in greater detail.

*(Continued)*

**Activity A** *(Continued)*                                      **Name** _____

1.  Analyze your Web page. What does your Web page say about your personality? _____

    _____

    _____

    _____

    _____

    _____

2.  Which personality traits have you inherited? _____

    _____

    _____

    _____

    _____

    _____

    _____

3.  Which personality traits have you acquired?_____

    _____

    _____

    _____

    _____

    _____

    _____

4.  What are your strongest personality traits? _____

    _____

    _____

    _____

    _____

    _____

    _____

5.  If you could change something about your personality, what would it be? _____

    _____

    _____

    _____

    _____

# Understanding Growth Patterns

**Activity B**

**Chapter 1**

Name _____

Date _____ Period _____

Answer the following questions concerning patterns of growth.

1. Define *chronological growth* using your own words. _____

   _____

   _____

2. How do you usually see teens portrayed in the media today? _____

   _____

   _____

   Do you feel this is accurate? Explain your answer. _____

   _____

   _____

3. How do you usually see older adults portrayed in the media today? _____

   _____

   _____

   Do you feel this is accurate? Explain your answer. _____

   _____

   _____

4. Define *physical growth* using your own words. _____

   _____

   _____

5. Summarize the differences in growth rate of boys and girls from 12 to 14 years of age.

   _____

   _____

   _____

   _____

6. Explain how physical growth can affect personality development. _____

   _____

   _____

   _____

   _____

*(Continued)*

**Activity B** (*Continued*)                    Name _____

7.  Define *intellectual growth* using your own words. _____
    _____
    _____

8.  Give an example of how the environment can influence intellectual growth. _____
    _____
    _____

9.  Define *emotional growth* using your own words. _____
    _____
    _____

10. Young people learn to manage or control their emotions during the teen years. What does this
    mean? _____
    _____
    _____
    _____
    _____
    _____

11. Define *social growth* using your own words._____
    _____
    _____

12. Certain social behaviors may be considered acceptable or unacceptable. Cite one behavior that is
    definitely considered unacceptable by your friends. _____
    _____
    _____

13. Define *philosophical growth* using your own words._____
    _____
    _____

14. What kinds of questions are you and your friends beginning to ask yourselves that indicate
    philosophical growth? _____
    _____
    _____
    _____
    _____
    _____

# Citizenship Interview

**Activity C**

**Chapter 1**

Name _____

Date _____ Period _____

Interview a veteran or an immigrant who has recently become a citizen of the United States. Find out the answers to the following questions. Share your responses with the class.

Person Interviewed: _____

What was your life like as a veteran or as an immigrant? _____

_____

_____

_____

_____

_____

How do you feel about the United States of America? _____

_____

_____

_____

_____

_____

What was a difficult time for you? _____

_____

_____

_____

_____

_____

What does being a citizen of the United States mean to you? _____

_____

_____

_____

_____

_____

What advice would you share with teens about how to be a good citizen? _____

_____

_____

_____

# Meeting Personal Expectations—Making a Difference

**Activity D**                           Name _____

**Chapter 1**                            Date _____ Period _____

Answer the following questions about your personal expectations in life and how you can make a difference in the world. Then imagine it is 20 years from now. Write an article about yourself describing your life, accomplishments, and difference you have made. Fill your name in the space for the headline.

What do you hope to accomplish in your future?_____

_____

_____

_____

Describe the career you hope to have. _____

_____

_____

_____

How will you make a difference in your community or the world? _____

_____

_____

_____

**Article:**_____ **Is Making a Difference**

_____

_____

_____

_____

_____

_____

_____

_____

# 2 Your Environment Affects Who You Are

## Environmental Influences

Activity A

Chapter 2

Name _____

Date _____ Period _____

Think about the environmental influences on your life. On the first ladder scale, rank the environmental factors listed below in order of their influence on your life now. On the second ladder scale, predict and rank the environmental factors in order of their influence on your life five years from now.

**Family, Peers, Education, Religion, Community**

Most influential now _____

_____

_____

_____

_____ Least influential now

Most influential in five years _____

_____

_____

_____

_____ Least influential in five years

# Influence of Birth Order

**Activity B**                                Name _____

**Chapter 2**                                Date _____ Period _____

The following phrases describe characteristics that are typical of oldest, middle, and youngest children. Decide which group of children each phrase describes and write *oldest*, *middle*, or *youngest* in the blanks provided. Then complete the following statement.

1. benefit from the companionship of a sibling

2. receive more direction from other family members

3. feel they need to care for younger siblings and set a good example for them

4. tend to be less independent

5. are often more independent

6. feel "overshadowed" at times by older or younger siblings

7. receive a lot of attention and protection from others in the family

8. grow up rapidly and tend to be given more responsibility

9. tend to be pampered or indulged as the "baby of the family"

10. have the strongest desire to achieve, as the parents may expect more

11. receive less encouragement to be independent

12. are often given less responsibility than an oldest child

1. _____

2. _____

3. _____

4. _____

5. _____

6. _____

7. _____

8. _____

9. _____

10. _____

11. _____

12. _____

The position I have in my family is that of _____. I can contribute positively to the environment of all family members by_____

_____

_____

_____

_____

_____

_____

_____

_____

# Family and Peer Influence

**Activity C**

**Chapter 2**

Name _____

Date _____ Period _____

The following chart lists activities that can be shared. Complete the chart, checking whether you would like to share the activity with your family, peers, or both. Add another activity you especially enjoy sharing with your family, peers, or both. Then answer the questions that follow.

| Activity | Prefer to Share with Family | Prefer to Share with Peers | Enjoy Sharing with Both Family and Peers |
|---|---|---|---|
| 1.  Going camping | | | |
| 2.  Bowling | | | |
| 3.  Watching TV | | | |
| 4.  Jogging | | | |
| 5.  Going to a concert | | | |
| 6.  Going to a religious function | | | |
| 7.  Going to a football game | | | |
| 8.  Shopping | | | |
| 9.  Talking about everyday matters | | | |
| 10.  Going to a movie | | | |
| 11.  Eating out | | | |
| 12. | | | |

Why do you prefer to share some activities only with your family and some activities only with your peers?

_____

_____

Explain how this might change as you get older. _____

_____

_____

# Media Watch

**Activity D**                                          Name _____

**Chapter 2**                                          Date _____ Period _____

Watch an episode of a family situation comedy on TV. While you view the program, make notes on the following. Be prepared to share your opinions of the show in class.

Name of program viewed: _____

1. Briefly summarize the plot of the program. What was the central problem, conflict, or issue, and how was it resolved? _____

   _____

   _____

   _____

   _____

   _____

2. What values (for example, honesty, hard work, caring) were reinforced in the program?

   _____

   _____

3. Were there any values that could have been reinforced but were not (for example, speaking respectfully to family members instead of "smarting off")? If so, what were they? _____

   _____

   _____

4. Summarize the central message you believe was being sent in this program (for example, "dishonesty doesn't pay" or "parents know best"). _____

   _____

   _____

   _____

5. Do you believe watching this show could influence a viewer's behavior in any way? Explain your answer. _____

   _____

   _____

   _____

   _____

   _____

   _____

   _____

# 3 You: Up Close and Personal

## Your Self-Concept

**Activity A**

**Chapter 3**

Name _____

Date _____ Period _____

Your self-concept is the way you see yourself. The following exercise will help you evaluate your self-concept. As you read each of the statements, place a check in the column that shows how often the statement describes your feelings: *Never, Sometimes, Most of the time,* or *All the time.* (There are no right or wrong answers.)

| | Never | Sometimes | Most of the time | All the time |
|---|---|---|---|---|
| _____ 1. I am uncomfortable when I meet new people. | | | | |
| _____ 2. I am glad I am who I am. | | | | |
| _____ 3. I enjoy daydreaming. | | | | |
| _____ 4. I am happy when my friends achieve what they want to achieve. | | | | |
| _____ 5. I am not satisfied with the way I look. | | | | |
| _____ 6. I find it easy to make decisions. | | | | |
| _____ 7. My classmates pick on me at school. | | | | |
| _____ 8. I finish anything I start. | | | | |
| _____ 9. When someone is wrong, I feel I must tell them. | | | | |
| _____ 10. I am truthful and dependable. | | | | |
| _____ 11. I am embarrassed when I am given a compliment. | | | | |
| _____ 12. I am not afraid to try something new even if there is a possibility I might not succeed. | | | | |
| _____ 13. The expectations my parents have of me are too high. | | | | |
| _____ 14. I choose my friends regardless of ethnic background or economic level. | | | | |
| _____ 15. I like to talk about other people. | | | | |
| _____ 16. I can handle new situations. | | | | |
| _____ 17. When someone embarrasses me, I try to get even with them. | | | | |
| _____ 18. I can be alone without feeling lonely or depressed. | | | | |
| _____ 19. I like to tell others about my possessions and accomplishments. | | | | |
| _____ 20. I feel confident even when others disagree with me. | | | | |

*(Continued)*

**Activity A** *(Continued)*        **Name**_____

On the blank line before each statement, place a zero for each time you checked *Never*. Place a 1 for each statement checked *Sometimes*, a 2 for *Most of the time*, and a 3 for *All the time*. Add the points for the odd-numbered statements and write the total in the blank below. Then add the points for the even-numbered statements and write the total in the blank below.

_____      A. Total of odd-numbered statements (1, 3, 5, 7, etc.)

_____      B. Total of even-numbered statements (2, 4, 6, 8, etc.)

If the number in B is greater than the number in A, you have a positive self-concept. If A is greater than B, your self-concept may be negative. Answer the following questions.

1. If you have a positive self-concept, what does this tell you about yourself? _____

_____

_____

_____

_____

_____

2. If you have a negative self-concept, what does this tell you about yourself? _____

_____

_____

_____

_____

_____

3. What can a person do to change a negative self-concept to a positive self-concept? _____

_____

_____

_____

_____

_____

_____

_____

_____

_____

# How Is Your Self-Esteem?

**Activity B**

**Chapter 3**

Name _____

Date _____ Period _____

Self-esteem is how you feel about yourself. The following exercise will help you evaluate your self-esteem. Below are 34 short sentences. Draw a circle around the sentences that describe how you feel most of the time. Then answer the questions that follow.

*I'm happy.   I'm talented.   I'm useless.   I'm sad.   I'm a loser.   I'm a winner.   I'm good looking.   I'm dumb.*

*I'm proud of myself.   I'm okay.   I'm dull.   I'm clumsy.   I'm sick a lot.   I'm bright.   I'm a gossip.   I'm weird.*

*I'm a bore.   I'm forgetful.   I have a positive attitude.   I'm cool.   I'm successful.   I'm afraid.   I'm lovable.*

*I'm healthy.   I'm concerned about others.   I'm adventuresome.   I'm shy.   I'm lively.   I'm a failure.   I'm friendly.*

*I'm tired.   I'm a good person.   I'm a pessimist.   I'm not really okay.*

1. Reread the sentences you circled above. What kind of picture do you get of yourself? _____

   _____

2. Choose one sentence above that contributes to low self-esteem. Explain what changes you could make to overcome this factor.

   Sentence chosen: _____

   Ways to overcome this factor: _____

   _____

   _____

3. Some days may go very well for you, and you feel really good about yourself. Your self-esteem will be very high on these days. List two relationships or events that might cause your sense of self-esteem to be high.

   A. _____

   B. _____

4. On other days, everything may seem to go wrong for you. Your sense of self-esteem may be lower on these days. List two relationships or events that might cause your sense of self-esteem to decrease.

   A. _____

   B. _____

5. Choose one of the relationships or events you listed in question 4 above. Describe how you could prevent this event or relationship from damaging your self-esteem.

   Relationship or event chosen: _____

   How you could prevent damage to your self-esteem: _____

   _____

   _____

# Character Traits

**Activity C**                             Name _____

**Chapter 3**                              Date _____ Period _____

Read the following list of positive character traits. Circle the ones you think are the most important. Choose one of these traits and answer the questions below.

| | | | |
|---|---|---|---|
| Reliable | Responsible | Self-disciplined | Careful |
| Considerate | Honorable | Dependable | Kind |
| Brave | Capable | Self-sufficient | Helpful |
| Honest | Thoughtful | Independent | Friendly |
| Generous | Hard-working | Sensitive | Strong-willed |
| Trustworthy | Discreet | Law-abiding | Punctual |

Character trait: _____

1. How would you describe a person with this character trait? _____

   _____

   _____

   _____

2. What experiences in a person's life might influence the development of this character trait? _____

   _____

   _____

   _____

   _____

   _____

3. What could a person do to develop this character trait? _____

   _____

   _____

   _____

   _____

   _____

   _____

   _____

   _____

# How Would You Respond?

**Activity D**

**Chapter 3**

Name _____

Date _____ Period _____

For each situation below, list the level of moral reasoning (preconventional, conventional, or postconventional) that is reflected based on Kohlberg's stages of moral development. Then write how you would respond to the situation—in some cases, by encouraging your friend to behave at a higher level.

1. You are shopping with a friend, and you see her shoplift a necklace from the store counter. She says, "Don't worry, we won't get caught."

   Level of moral reasoning: _____

   The best way to respond: _____

   _____

   _____

   _____

   _____

2. On your way home from school, you and your friends notice some younger children taunting and teasing a first-grader. Your friends put a stop to it and comfort the child. When you ask your friends why they intervened, one friend replies, "I did what I thought was right. I could not stand by and watch a young child suffering at the hands of a bunch of bullies."

   Level of moral reasoning: _____

   The best way to respond: _____

   _____

   _____

   _____

   _____

3. You and your friend are shopping for antiques at a yard sale, and she sees a rare item that is worth $200. The owner, who does not know of its worth, has marked the price as $15. Your friend pays the $15 and gloats all the way home about her "bargain." When you object, she says, "It was a perfectly legal transaction."

   Level of moral reasoning: _____

   The best way to respond: _____

   _____

   _____

   _____

   _____

*(Continued)*

**Activity D** *(Continued)*                              **Name**_____

4. You and your friend are servers in a local restaurant. You report all of the tips you make as income on your income tax form, but your friend does not. When you ask her about it, she says, "They won't check, and I won't get caught."

   Level of moral reasoning: _____

   The best way to respond:_____

   _____

   _____

   _____

   _____

5. Your friend is at a party, and someone tells an untrue and damaging story about a mutual friend. Instead of countering the story, your friend pretends she did not hear it. When you ask her why, she says, "I didn't say anything because I was afraid that if I did, the person who told the story wouldn't like me."

   Level of moral reasoning: _____

   The best way to respond:_____

   _____

   _____

   _____

   _____

6. Your friend has been having difficulty writing a term paper for a class assignment. Another friend has offered to write it for him, but he refuses, saying, "My paper might not be the greatest in the world, but I believe honesty is the best policy. At least what I turn in will be my own work."

   Level of moral reasoning: _____

   The best way to respond:_____

   _____

   _____

   _____

   _____

# Defense Mechanisms

**Activity E**

**Chapter 3**

Name _____

Date _____ Period _____

Various defense mechanisms are listed below. Read the following situations. Then write the name of the defense mechanism described by each situation.

| | | |
|---|---|---|
| compensation | displacement | rationalization |
| conversion | giving up | regression |
| daydreaming | idealization | |
| direct attack | projection | |

1. Emily auditioned for the lead in the musical at school. When her name did not appear on the cast list, she said, "I'll never try out for another play."

   _____

2. When Josh is bored in history class, he lets his imagination take him to the beach where he surfs the big waves.

   _____

3. Tamica misses her brother's birthday party to go to the mall where she hopes to run into the popular girls from school.

   _____

4. Mohan is angry because his parents have told him he must clean the garage instead of going to the movies. He stomps off to his room and slams the door.

   _____

5. Whenever Miko has a math test, she gets an upset stomach.

   _____

6. Malcolm got a bad grade on a test. When he got home from school, he yelled at his sister when she smiled at him.

   _____

7. Saba is carrying her lunch tray in the cafeteria. When she turns her head to talk to Joel, she runs into Mike, spilling both their lunches. She blames Mike, saying, "Why didn't you get out of my way? Now you've ruined our lunches."

   _____

8. Colin got cut from the basketball team because he was always late for practices. He said, "That's okay, I have better things to do with my time and the coach didn't like me anyway."

   _____

9. Julia did not make the volleyball team. However, she made the cross country team where she became captain of the team.

   _____

10. When Vincent got a new hairstyle, Jaden asked, "Did they cut your hair with a lawnmower?" Vincent responded by saying, "I heard your four-year-old sister cuts yours."

    _____

# Attitudes

Name _____

Date _____ Period _____

The teens in the following situations have negative attitudes that influence their behavior. Read each situation and explain how each person might respond if he or she had a more positive attitude.

1. Matt tends to overgeneralize by viewing a negative event as part of an endless pattern of defeat. When he was caught going over the speed limit, he was sure he was receiving the first of many tickets. "After all," he said, "teens are always going to be the target of the cops." If Matt had a more positive attitude, he might _____

_____

_____

_____

2. Tanya jumps to conclusions, assuming other people are critical of her. She applied for several part-time jobs after school, but they were all given to other applicants. "The employers must all think I won't be a good worker," she said. If Tanya had a more positive attitude, she might

_____

_____

_____

3. Janelle blows things way out of proportion. She struck out at bat in the last game and her team lost. Now she thinks she will be blamed for an entire losing season. If Janelle had a more positive attitude, she might _____

_____

_____

_____

4. Dennis allows negative emotions to take over. He was trying out for a part in the school play when he suddenly felt very dejected. He had never been given an important part in a play. He felt he was not as talented as the other people at the tryouts. He was certain he would not have a chance for the part. If Dennis had a more positive attitude, he might_____

_____

_____

_____

5. Liam takes personal blame for events for which he is not entirely responsible. He and his friends were playing Frisbee™ in the park when one of his friends threw the Frisbee into a crowd of people. His friends ran off and he was left to be reprimanded for not paying attention to what he was doing. He left the park blaming himself. If Liam had a more positive attitude, he might

_____

_____

_____

# 4 Your Decisions

## Values

Name _____

Date _____ Period _____

In the two columns at the left, check the values you consider most important. In the right column, rank those you checked in order of priority. Then answer the questions that follow.

| | | |
|---|---|---|
| _____ Independent | _____ Courageous | _____ Most important |
| _____ Cheerful | _____ Philosophical | _____ |
| _____ Self-controlled | _____ Forgiving | _____ |
| _____ Honest | _____ Flexible | _____ |
| _____ Athletic | _____ Polite | _____ |
| _____ Intellectual | _____ Easygoing | _____ (You may not use all these blanks, or you may want to add some more.) |
| _____ Responsible | _____ Imaginative | _____ |
| _____ Ambitious | _____ Logical | _____ |
| _____ Broad-minded | _____ Outgoing | _____ |
| _____ Decisive | _____ Loving | _____ |
| | | _____ |
| | | _____ |
| | | _____ Least important |

1. How have your values changed since your childhood? _____

_____

_____

2. How do you think your values may change when you reach middle age? _____

_____

_____

3. How do you think your values may change when you reach old age? _____

_____

_____

# Understanding Your Values

**Activity B**                    Name _____

**Chapter 4**                     Date _____ Period _____

Answer the following questions related to your values.

1. The thing I like best about our school is _____

   _____

   _____

2. The thing I would like most to change about our school is _____

   _____

   _____

3. The personality characteristic I like most in my friends is_____

   _____

4. The time of day I like best is _____

5. When it is raining, I like to _____

   _____

6. In five years, I think I will be _____

   _____

   _____

7. If I could change one aspect of my physical appearance, it would be ____

   _____

   _____

8. When I am 60 years old, I think I will feel like_____

   _____

   _____

9. If I could meet any person in the world today, I would like to meet ____

   _____

   _____

10. One thing that really makes me angry is _____

   _____

   _____

11. One thing I really enjoy is _____

   _____

   _____

12. One thing I hope to accomplish in my life is _____

   _____

   _____

# How Values Influence Decisions

**Activity C**

**Chapter 4**

Name _____

Date _____ Period _____

How you might handle each of the following situations is influenced by your values. Explain how you would react in each situation and how your values would influence that decision. Then share your responses in a small group. Role-play one of the situations for the class.

1. You are trying to decide what you will do on a date next Friday night. _____

   _____

   _____

   _____

   _____

   _____

   _____

2. You are walking down the street with your friends, and you see a wallet that has evidently been lost by someone. _____

   _____

   _____

   _____

   _____

   _____

   _____

3. You are in a store shopping with some friends, and one of them suggests it would be easy to walk out with a small item without paying for it. _____

   _____

   _____

   _____

   _____

   _____

Group's ideas for role-playing scene:

_____

_____

_____

_____

_____

# Your Time/Life Line

**Activity D**

**Chapter 4**

Name _____

Date _____ Period _____

Plot your goals for your life on the time/life line below using different colored pencils or markers. Some of your goals will overlap. Then write a brief summary of your goals. Compare the timing and sequences of your goals with those of your classmates.

## Time/Life Line

| Goals: | 0 | 10 | 20 | 30 | 40 | 50 | 60 | 70 | 80 | 90 | |
|---|---|---|---|---|---|---|---|---|---|---|---|
| **Student** | | | | | | | | | | | |
| **Part-time worker** | | | | | | | | | | | |
| **Full-time worker** | | | | | | | | | | | |
| **Spouse** | | | | | | | | | | | |
| **Parent/Grandparent** | | | | | | | | | | | |
| **Retiree** | | | | | | | | | | | |
| **Other goals (describe)** | | | | | | | | | | | |
| | | | | | | | | | | | |
| | | | | | | | | | | | |

Summary:

_____

_____

_____

_____

_____

_____

_____

_____

_____

_____

_____

_____

_____

_____

_____

_____

# Identifying Your Resources

**Activity E**

**Chapter 4**

Name _____

Date _____ Period _____

In order to reach your goals, you will need to use human resources (which come from within a person) and nonhuman resources (which come from outside a person). In the first column, write a goal of yours. In the second column, write one or more human resources that you can use to reach your goal. In the third column, write one or more nonhuman resources that you can use to reach your goal. Continue the exercise using other goals. An example is provided below.

| Goal | Human Resources | Nonhuman Resources |
|---|---|---|
| Lose 5 pounds | Personal will power<br>Ability to plan low-calorie meals<br>Time for physical activity | Bicycle<br>Running shoes<br>Community fitness facilities |
|  |  |  |
|  |  |  |
|  |  |  |

# Using the Decision-Making Process

**Activity F**                                   Name _____

**Chapter 4**                                    Date _____ Period _____

Think of a decision you must make. Follow the steps in the decision-making process to determine the best alternative.

Step 1: Identify the decision to be made.

_____

_____

Step 2: List three possible alternatives.

_____

_____

Step 3: Evaluate the consequences of each alternative.

#1 Pros:_____        #1 Cons: _____

_____                _____

_____                _____

#2 Pros:_____        #2 Cons: _____

_____                _____

_____                _____

#3 Pros:_____        #3 Cons: _____

_____                _____

_____                _____

Step 4: Choose the best alternative.

_____

Step 5: Describe how you will act on your decision.

_____

_____

_____

Step 6: Evaluate your decision.

_____

_____

_____

# 5 Your Future Career Decisions

## Clues to Your Career Choice

**Activity A**

**Chapter 5**

Name _____

Date _____ Period _____

Factors that should enter into the choice of a career include personal interests, values, aptitudes, and abilities. Answering the following questions will help you identify careers that may be of interest to you.

1. Do you like to work with people or do you prefer to work with objects or information?

   _____

   List six jobs that sound interesting to you based on how you answered this question.

   A. _____

   B. _____

   C. _____

   D. _____

   E. _____

   F. _____

2. Do you prefer dealing with abstract concepts (time, space, ideas) or do you prefer working with concrete objects (motors, power tools, computers)? _____

   Which of the six jobs you listed above would still be of interest to you based on how you answered this question?

   A. _____

   B. _____

   C. _____

   D. _____

3. What are some of your aptitudes (special talents) and abilities? _____

   _____

   _____

   _____

   _____

   _____

   _____

*(Continued)*

**Activity A** *(Continued)*                     **Name**_____

Which of the jobs you listed in answer to the previous question would you be good at based on how you answered this question?

A. _____

B. _____

C. _____

4. What types of leisure activities do you enjoy?_____

_____

_____

_____

_____

What careers do these leisure activities indicate you might enjoy? _____

_____

_____

_____

_____

_____

5. What subjects have been easiest for you in school? _____

_____

_____

_____

_____

What careers that you have listed above are related to these subjects? _____

_____

_____

_____

_____

6. Review your answers to previous questions. What career might be the best choice for you? Explain your answer. _____

_____

_____

_____

_____

# Combining Work with School

**Activity B**                                       Name _____

**Chapter 5**                                       Date _____ Period _____

You may want to work part-time while you continue your education. The following activity will help you with this decision. If you are already working, it may help you evaluate the decision you made to combine work with school. Complete the sentences below and answer the questions on the following page.

**If I work part-time,**

the hours I spend on my job will be…

_____

_____

my transportation needs will be…

_____

_____

my clothing needs will be…

_____

_____

my health concerns will be…

_____

_____

my family will be…

_____

_____

my participation in school activities will be…

_____

_____

my social life will be…

_____

_____

my school assignments will be…

_____

_____

*(Continued)*

**Activity B** *(Continued)*                    **Name** _____

**Do I have what it takes to be a good employee?**

Can I follow directions? _____

Am I considerate of others? _____

Can I handle criticism? _____

Can I get along with other people? _____

Can I work with speed as well as accuracy? _____

Am I punctual and dependable? _____

Can I work under pressure? _____

Is my appearance neat and clean? _____

Do I mind taking orders? _____

**My goals**

for the short term are…

_____

_____

for the long term are…

_____

_____

for my future career are…

_____

_____

Will a part-time job help me achieve my goals? _____

_____

_____

_____

Reviewing what I have written, I feel I (should/should not) look for a part-time job because_____

_____

_____

_____

_____

_____

_____

_____

_____

# Workplace Skills

**Activity C**

**Chapter 5**

Name _____

Date _____ Period _____

Evaluate your workplace skills by responding to each of the following statements according to the way it describes you. Mark **A** for always, **S** for sometimes, and **N** for never. Score your responses by following the directions below.

_____ I am able to make decisions easily.

_____ I have confidence in myself.

_____ I like to accept new challenges.

_____ I enjoy working with others.

_____ I like to complete projects I start.

_____ I am able to respond to the needs of others.

_____ I like to solve problems.

_____ I can sacrifice personal goals in order to reach group goals.

_____ I am a good listener.

_____ I am able to stand up for my convictions.

_____ I enjoy speaking in front of a group.

_____ I can resist unreasonable demands made by others.

_____ I am able to influence others.

_____ I am able to stimulate and encourage others to achieve group goals.

_____ I consider all alternatives carefully when making decisions.

_____ I am able to follow through when difficult decisions have been made.

_____ I am willing to share responsibility with others rather than do everything myself.

_____ I am quick to praise others for their achievements.

_____ I am able to communicate clearly.

_____ I like to coordinate ideas, plans, and people.

Give yourself two points for each response marked **A** and one point for each response marked **S**. Add up your total points. If you scored 35 or more, you have very good workplace skills; 30–34, you have workplace potential; 25–29, you have many skills that will help you succeed in the workplace; 24 or less, you may need to work on your workplace skills.

_____ **A** responses × 2 = _____

_____ **S** responses × 1 = _____

Total Score _____

How can you improve your workplace skills?

_____

_____

_____

_____

# Write Your Résumé

**Activity D**                                      Name _____

**Chapter 5**                                       Date _____ Period _____

Draft a résumé based on the outline below. After you have finished, exchange your résumé with another member of your class and obtain his or her comments and suggestions. Revise as necessary.

Name _____

Address _____

Telephone _____

E-mail _____

Job Objective _____

_____

Education _____

_____

_____

_____

_____

Work Experience* Dates            Place of work and description of responsibilities

_____

_____

_____

_____

_____

_____

_____

Activities and Honors

_____

_____

_____

Hobbies

_____

_____

_____

References available upon request.

*Students who have no formal work experience may wish to include volunteer work or list special skills instead of work experience.

# Ask Molly Mentor

**Activity E**                    Name _____

**Chapter 5**                     Date _____ Period _____

Imagine that you are a newspaper advice columnist called *Molly Mentor*. Your job is to advise readers who write to you about their job issues and problems. Write your advice in the spaces provided below.

*Dear Molly Mentor,*

*My supervisor is a "control freak." Whenever she assigns me work, she stands over me to make sure I do it correctly. Sometimes she makes me so nervous that I make mistakes. Do you have any advice?*

*Nervous*

Dear Nervous,

_____

_____

_____

_____

M.M.


*Dear Molly Mentor,*

*I work in a cubicle and try hard to avoid disturbing others. However, two coworkers sometimes forget that others are trying to focus on their work. One of them likes to carry on long, personal telephone conversations in a loud voice. Another likes to play loud music on her radio. This is interfering with my ability to do my job, but I need to get along with them. Do you have any suggestions?*

*Distracted*

Dear Distracted,

_____

_____

_____

_____

M.M.


*Dear Molly Mentor,*

*I enjoy my job and like the feeling that comes with putting in a good day's work. However, one of my coworkers stops by my desk several times a day for lengthy personal chats. As a result, it is hard for me to get my work done. Sometimes I think I should tell this person how I feel, but I am afraid of making her mad. Any thoughts on what I should do?*

*Talked Out*

*(Continued)*

**Activity E** *(Continued)*                          **Name** _____

Dear Talked Out,

_____

_____

_____

_____

M.M.


*Dear Molly Mentor,*

*I was hired by someone who liked my work, but this person retired. I think my new boss is trying to get rid of me so she can give my job to a friend of hers. She knows that she has no grounds for firing me because I work hard and do well. However, she is giving me so much work with impossible deadlines that I think she is setting me up to fail. Then she will have grounds for letting me go. What should I do?*

*Unhappy*

Dear Unhappy,

_____

_____

_____

_____

M.M.


*Dear Molly Mentor,*

*I made a big mistake by getting involved romantically with a coworker. At first, I hoped that we might get married someday, but later I knew this could never happen. Ever since I broke off our relationship, I have avoided this person. Now we have to see each other at meetings several times a week. This person is making a point of refusing to speak to me at these meetings. What should I do?*

*Worried*

Dear Worried,

_____

_____

_____

_____

M.M.

# 6 Your Health Decisions

## Your Nutrition/Physical Activity Inventory

**Activity A**

**Chapter 6**

Name_____

Date _____ Period _____

How healthful is your lifestyle? In the following activity, read each of the statements concerning nutrition and physical activity. Circle the number on the scale that best describes your health practices. Then total your score.

| | 4 | 3 | 2 | 1 | 0 |
|---|---|---|---|---|---|
| **Fat** | I eat poultry/fish more often than red meat. | | I eat red meat three to four times per week; poultry/fish less often. | | I eat red meat every day; seldom eat poultry/fish. |
| **Fat** | I drink skim milk; rarely eat ice cream, butter, or cheese. | | I drink lowfat milk; eat butter, cheese, and ice cream three to four times a week. | | I drink whole milk or no milk at all; cheese, butter, and ice cream daily. |
| **Salt** | I never add salt to food at the table; never eat salty snacks. | | I occasionally use salt on food; frequently eat salty snacks. | | I almost always use salt on food; eat several salty snacks daily. |
| **Balanced Diet** | I eat a wide variety of foods from each of the food groups daily. | | I sometimes eat foods from each of the food groups; occasionally I eat too many fats and starches. | | I seldom eat foods from each of the food groups; often eat fats and starches. |
| **Fiber** | I eat whole-grain bread/cereals and fresh fruits/vegetables daily. | | I eat whole-grain breads/cereals and fresh fruits/vegetables about three times a week. | | I never eat whole-grain breads/ cereals and seldom eat fresh fruits/vegetables. |

*(Continued)*

**Activity A** (Continued)                                        Name _____

| | | 4 | 3 | 2 | 1 | 0 |
|---|---|---|---|---|---|---|
| **Weight** | | I am within the ideal weight range for my height. | | I am about 10 pounds over/ under my ideal weight range. | | I am more than 25 pounds over/ under my ideal weight range. |
| | | (Height/weight charts can be found online and in nutrition textbooks.) | | | | |
| **Calories** | | 4 | 3 | 2 | 1 | 0 |
| | | I am careful to select low-calorie foods. | | I usually choose low-calorie foods, but splurge on high-calorie desserts several times a week. | | I always seem to eat high-calorie foods. |
| **Physical Activity** | | 4 | 3 | 2 | 1 | 0 |
| | | I am involved in vigorous physical activities almost every day. | | I participate in physical activities about two to three times each week. | | I do not participate in physical activities at all. |

My total score is _____.

What your score means:

0-8    You are making decisions that are not beneficial to your health. The practices on the right side of each scale have been linked to serious diseases, such as high blood pressure, diabetes, and heart disease. You can improve your health by following the practices listed to the left in the inventory. Make a conscious effort to improve your health practices and score yourself again at the end of the month.

9-16    Many teens may fall in this category. Continuing your present nutrition and physical activity practices could lead to health problems as you mature. You need to try to improve your health practices. Review your health practices and score yourself again at the end of the month.

17-24    You are making many decisions that are good for your health. Teens in this category will probably have fewer health risks than those with lower scores. Continue to follow these good health practices and see if you can score even higher at the end of the month!

25-32    You have chosen a healthful lifestyle, and you will have less risk of serious illness as you enter adulthood. Maintain these practices and be a model for other teens and your family. Keep up the good work!

# Nutrition Log

**Activity B**

**Chapter 6**

Name _____

Date _____ Period _____

Record everything you eat for three days on the chart on the next page. Include all snacks and beverages. Then total the amounts you included from each food group in MyPyramid each day. Analyze each day's diet following the recommendations found at www.MyPyramid.gov for your age, gender, and activity level. Record those recommendations below.

_____ grains

_____ vegetables

_____ fruits

_____ milk

_____ meat and beans

Answer the questions about your eating habits below.

1. Were there any food groups that you were lacking in all three days? _____

    _____

    _____

    _____

2. Were there any food groups you were including too often in your diet? _____

    _____

    _____

    _____

    _____

3. Were you skipping some meals altogether? _____

    _____

    _____

4. Were you eating too many foods that are not included in MyPyramid? If so, what were they and how might this affect your health? _____

    _____

    _____

    _____

    _____

5. What specific plans can you make to improve your diet? _____

    _____

    _____

    _____

*(Continued)*

**Activity B** *(Continued)*                          Name _____

| | Day 1 | Day 2 | Day 3 |
|---|---|---|---|
| **Breakfast** | | | |
| **Lunch** | | | |
| **Dinner** | | | |
| **Snacks** | | | |
| **Totals** | _____ Grains<br>_____ Vegetables<br>_____ Fruits<br>_____ Milk<br>_____ Meat and beans | _____ Grains<br>_____ Vegetables<br>_____ Fruits<br>_____ Milk<br>_____ Meat and beans | _____ Grains<br>_____ Vegetables<br>_____ Fruits<br>_____ Milk<br>_____ Meat and beans |
| **Analysis** | | | |

# Weight Control

**Activity C**

**Chapter 6**

Name _____

Date _____ Period _____

Many teens want to lose weight. Some may wish to gain weight. In the following activity, analyze your eating habits and goals for weight control.

1. Determine the number of calories you should consume each day to maintain your present weight.*

   I need _____ calories each day to maintain my weight.

2. Refer to your record of foods eaten for three days in Activity B. Using a calorie chart, determine your calorie intake for each of the three days.*

   _____ calories on day 1

   _____ calories on day 2

   _____ calories on day 3

   Total calories for three days _____

   Divide the total by three and enter below.

   My average daily calorie intake is _____ calories.

3. Compare the number of calories you should eat to maintain your weight with the number of calories you are actually eating. If you continue to consume this many calories each day, will you gain or lose weight?

   I will _____ weight.

4. Refer to height/weight charts to determine if you are overweight or underweight.* If you fall within the normal weight range, decide for yourself if you would like to gain or lose a few pounds.

   I would like to (gain, lose) _____ pounds.

5. Review your daily intake of food in Activity B. How can you revise your eating habits to either gain or lose weight and still meet your nutritional needs? Discuss your plans below.

   In order to (gain, lose) _____ weight, I need to make the following changes in my eating habits:

   _____

   _____

   _____

   _____

   _____

   _____

*Refer to charts that can be found in foods and nutrition textbooks provided by your teacher.

# My Physical Activity Inventory

**Activity D**                                          Name _____

**Chapter 6**                                          Date _____ Period _____

A regular program of physical activity can help you feel good—physically and mentally. In the chart below, record the amount of time you spent in physical activity during the past week. Include only vigorous, conditioning physical activity. List the approximate number of minutes spent in each activity.

| Physical Activities: | M | T | W | Th | F | Sat | Sun |
|---|---|---|---|---|---|---|---|
| Aerobics | | | | | | | |
| Jogging | | | | | | | |
| Competitive sports | | | | | | | |
| P.E. class | | | | | | | |
| Swimming | | | | | | | |
| Tennis | | | | | | | |
| Other: | | | | | | | |
| Total | | | | | | | |

The ideal fitness program includes some physical activity every day. A good physical activity program includes 60 minutes of moderate to vigorous physical activity every day. It should also include warm-up and cool-down activities. Considering these guidelines, analyze your physical activity program. Then describe how you could improve your physical activity plan.

Analysis of your current physical activity program:

_____

_____

_____

_____

_____

_____

How could you improve your physical activity program? _____

_____

_____

_____

_____

_____

_____

# Stress Rating Scale

Activity E

Chapter 6

Name _____

Date _____ Period _____

The following chart lists events that may cause stress in the life of a teen. Working in small groups, think of additional events that can add stress to teen lives. An example might be breaking up with a boyfriend or girlfriend. Remember that stress can occur from positive events as well. Share your ideas with the entire class. Decide on a point value for each event you add to the list.

| Life Event | Point Value | Your Score |
|---|---|---|
| Death of a parent | 100 | _____ |
| Divorce of parents | 73 | _____ |
| Separation of parents | 65 | _____ |
| Death of close family member | 63 | _____ |
| Personal injury or illness | 53 | _____ |
| Marriage | 50 | _____ |
| Fired from job | 47 | _____ |
| Marital reconciliation | 45 | _____ |
| Change in health of family member | 44 | _____ |
| Pregnancy | 40 | _____ |
| Gain of new family member (birth, adoption, grandparent moving in, etc.) | 29 | _____ |
| Change in financial state (better or worse off than usual) | 38 | _____ |
| Death of a close friend | 37 | _____ |
| Change to a different line of work | 36 | _____ |
| Change in responsibilities at work (promotion, demotion) | 29 | _____ |
| Outstanding personal achievement | 28 | _____ |
| Begin or end school | 26 | _____ |
| Revision of personal habits (dress, manners, associations) | 24 | _____ |
| Trouble with boss | 23 | _____ |
| Change in work hours or conditions | 20 | _____ |
| Change in residence | 20 | _____ |
| Change in schools | 20 | _____ |
| Change in recreation | 19 | _____ |
| Change in religious activities | 19 | _____ |
| Change in social activities (clubs, dancing, movies) | 18 | _____ |
| Change in sleeping habits | 16 | _____ |
| Change in eating habits (more or less food, different hours or surroundings) | 15 | _____ |
| Vacation | 13 | _____ |
| Christmas or other major holiday | 12 | _____ |
| Minor violations of the law (traffic ticket, disturbing the peace) | 11 | _____ |

**Additional teen life events:**

_____

_____

*(Continued)*

**Activity E** *(Continued)*     **Name**_____

Using the scale on the preceding page and the additional events your class added to the list, determine your stress points. Write the point value on the line for those events that occurred in your life over the past year. If an event occurred more than once during the year, multiply the point value by the number of times the event occurred. Write that amount on the line. Add your total score and record below.

Total stress points:_____

If you scored over 200 points, you have experienced a high level of stress during the past year. Think about how you handled the more stressful events. Describe below how you managed the stress created by one of these events.

Describe the event:_____

_____

_____

_____

_____

_____

_____

How did you manage the stress created by this event?_____

_____

_____

_____

_____

_____

What other techniques could you have used to handle the stress?_____

_____

_____

_____

_____

_____

# 7 Avoiding Harmful Substances

## Smoking

**Activity A**

**Chapter 7**

Name _____

Date _____ Period _____

1. Place the letters in the blanks to rank the reasons people decide to smoke (in your opinion):

   (A) Makes them look older. (B) Allows them to join a peer group. (C) Relaxes them. (D) Gives them something to do with their hands. (E) Their parents, brothers, or sisters smoked. (F) Makes them feel good. (G) Lets them kill time when bored. (H) Helps them cope with problems. (I) Way to get back at parents or authority figures who are telling them not to smoke.

   Most influential _____

   _____

   _____

   _____

   _____

   _____

   _____

   _____ Least influential

2. If a person has developed a smoking habit, what would you consider to be the most successful way to break that habit? Place the letters in the blanks to indicate your response.

   (A) Cut down slowly, then quit. (B) Smoke low-nicotine, low-tar cigarettes. (C) Substitute candy or chewing gum. (D) Attend counseling groups. (E) Receive hypnosis to stop habit. (F) Decide to stop and never have another cigarette. (G) Buy special commercial products designed to help people quit.

   Most successful _____

   _____

   _____

   _____

   _____

   _____ Least successful

*(Continued)*

**Activity A** *(Continued)*                                    **Name** _____

3.  What does it cost to smoke? List the price of one pack of cigarettes.

    Cost if you smoke: 1 pack per day _____ × 365 days = _____

    2 packs per day × 365 days = _____

    Cost of smoking 1 pack per day for:  one year _____  two years _____  five years _____

    10 years _____  20 years _____  40 years _____

    List the approximate cost of three items you wish you could afford in the next year. Compare these with the costs of smoking for one year.

    _____  _____  _____

    How do you want to spend your money? _____

    List the approximate cost of one item you wish you could afford in five years. _____ Could you afford this item if you did *not* smoke for five years? _____

4.  If you could vote for a law banning the sale of tobacco, how would you vote?

    I would vote to ban the sale of tobacco because _____

    _____

    I would vote to allow the sale of tobacco because_____

    _____

5.  Nonsmoking areas must now be designated in many public places. In some places, smoking is banned altogether. Briefly describe what is being done in your community in restaurants, businesses, and other public places.

    _____

    _____

    _____

    _____

    _____

    _____

6.  Do you agree or disagree with the current trend to not allow smoking in certain areas? Explain your answer.

    _____

    _____

    _____

    _____

    _____

    _____

# Drinking and Driving

**Activity B**

**Chapter 7**

Name _____

Date _____ Period _____

Respond to the following statements. Then discuss these statements in class.

**Agree   Disagree   Unsure**

_____ _____ _____   1.   If you have one or two drinks, you can drive just as well as you can without having anything to drink.

_____ _____ _____   2.   The experienced driver is rarely bothered by a few drinks.

_____ _____ _____   3.   The law should limit the amount of alcohol served to a person who drives to a bar.

_____ _____ _____   4.   I would feel safe riding with a driver who had recovered from alcoholism.

_____ _____ _____   5.   Often the relaxing effect of a drink can improve driving.

_____ _____ _____   6.   A person convicted of driving while intoxicated should have his or her license revoked.

_____ _____ _____   7.   Tests to determine blood alcohol levels should be required of suspected drinking drivers.

_____ _____ _____   8.   It is okay to drive after a few drinks, but it is not okay to drive after many drinks.

_____ _____ _____   9.   Not enough arrests are made for driving while intoxicated.

_____ _____ _____   10.  Arrests for driving under the influence of alcohol should carry a heavy fine.

_____ _____ _____   11.  Most people are more cautious behind the wheel after drinking.

_____ _____ _____   12.  When hosting a party, the amount of alcoholic beverages served to driving guests should be limited.

_____ _____ _____   13.  Not driving after drinking is the most desirable behavior.

_____ _____ _____   14.  Driving while intoxicated (DWI) is a community problem as well as an individual problem.

_____ _____ _____   15.  People should not make fun of or pressure those who choose not to drink.

_____ _____ _____   16.  If necessary, I would attempt to prevent others from driving if their driving ability had been impaired by alcohol.

_____ _____ _____   17.  If necessary, I would attempt to prevent others from riding as passengers with a driver whose ability had been impaired by alcohol.

_____ _____ _____   18.  I would support measures such as legislation, enforcement, education, and engineering that would reduce the DUI (driving under the influence) problem.

# Alcohol's Effect on Personal Relationships

**Activity C**

**Chapter 7**

Name _____

Date _____ Period _____

Write your reactions to the following situations about relationship problems caused by drinking. (Girls write about problems 1 and 3. Boys write about problems 2 and 4.) Then divide into small groups to discuss reactions. (Each small group should include both girls and boys.)

1. Consider the problems that arise when a girl is dating a boy who has a drinking problem. For instance, if the boy ignores her wishes and continues to drink at a party, should she leave without him? If they leave together, should she insist on driving? Should she ignore him and have a good time herself? Should she feel obligated to see that he arrives home safely?

   _____

   _____

   _____

   _____

2. Consider the problems that arise when a boy is dating a girl who has a drinking problem. For instance, should he try to influence the girl to stop drinking? Should he feel responsible for seeing that none of her drinks contain alcohol? If she is drinking too much at a party, should he try to suggest that he take her home early? Should he ignore her and have a good time himself? Should he feel obligated to see that she arrives home safely?

   _____

   _____

   _____

   _____

3. Consider the problems that arise when a young wife has a drinking problem. Should the husband try to influence his wife to stop drinking? Should he tell their relatives or her coworkers that she has a drinking problem? Should he still show affection to his wife, or should he ignore her if she continues to drink? Should he try to influence her to seek help? Should he try to control sources of alcohol in her life?

   _____

   _____

   _____

   _____

4. Consider the problems that arise when a young husband has a drinking problem. Should the wife try to influence her husband to stop drinking? Should she tell their relatives or his coworkers that he has a drinking problem? Should she still show affection to her husband, or should she ignore him if he continues to drink? Should she try to influence him to seek help? Should she try to control sources of alcohol in his life?

   _____

   _____

   _____

   _____

# The Use of Alcohol

**Activity D**

**Chapter 7**

Name _____

Date _____ Period _____

1. Place the letters in the blanks to rank the following, indicating your answer to the following statement: "I think drinking would be the most difficult to say no to when a teen is…"

    (A) driving (B) dining in a restaurant (C) emotionally upset (D) at home alone (E) at a party (F) with a group of other teens who are drinking

    Most difficult _____

    _____

    _____

    _____

    _____

    _____ Least difficult

2. If you were at a party and you knew "spiked" punch was being served, would you drink the punch in order to go along with the crowd?

    Yes, because _____

    No, because _____

    What are the dangers of "spiked" punch? _____

    _____

3. If the person who drove you to a party was drinking heavily, would you ask someone else to take you home, or would you feel you had to go home with the person who brought you?

    I would let someone else take me home because _____

    _____

    I would go home with the person who brought me because _____

    _____

    I would drive the car home myself, but ask a friend to take my date home because _____

    _____

4. If you were with a group of friends and they decided to play a drinking game, what would you do?

    _____ Assume a superior attitude and refuse to drink.

    _____ Say "No, thank you," and say nothing to those who are drinking.

    _____ Drink a little and pretend to be enjoying it.

    _____ Keep up with the crowd.

    _____ Excuse yourself and find a way home.

    _____ Other: _____

*(Continued)*

**Activity D** *(Continued)*        **Name** _____

5. Alcohol can change a person's behavior and personality.

   I agree/disagree because_____

   _____

6. The fact that young people see adults and famous people drink affects their decisions about using alcohol.

   I agree/disagree because_____

   _____

7. Place the letters in the blanks to rank the following, indicating your answer to the following statement: "If I felt I had a drinking problem, the first person I would consult would be…"

   (A) religious leader (B) parents (C) friends (D) physician (E) member of Alcoholics Anonymous (F) school counselor (G) member of Students Against Destructive Decisions (SADD), if available

   First to consult _____

   _____

   _____

   _____

   _____

   _____

   _____ Last to consult

8. Recent community response to the alcohol problem has prompted such activities as these: formation of SADD chapters; bars offering breath tests to determine driving ability; cab companies offering to drive people home who are unable to drive; in all states, tougher DUI laws, and tougher laws to control false I.D.s.

   What other activities have been initiated in response to the alcohol problem? _____

   _____

   Write a short paragraph indicating which of these you feel is the most effective. _____

   _____

   _____

   _____

   _____

   _____

   _____

   _____

   _____

   _____

   _____

# How Alcohol Is Portrayed on Television

**Activity E**

**Chapter 7**

Name _____

Date _____ Period _____

Watch television for a total of two hours. Use the form below to record how alcohol is shown or mentioned. Be sure to pay attention to commercials as well as programs.

| Time period | Program | Commercial | Network/station | Positive or negative reference | Beer, wine, or liquor |
|---|---|---|---|---|---|
|  |  |  |  |  |  |
|  |  |  |  |  |  |
|  |  |  |  |  |  |
|  |  |  |  |  |  |
|  |  |  |  |  |  |
|  |  |  |  |  |  |

How do you feel the attention to alcohol on television influences people's use of alcohol? _____

_____

_____

_____

# Saying No to Alcohol

**Activity F**

**Chapter 7**

Name _____

Date _____ Period _____

For each of the following situations, write ways to say no to alcohol. Then compare answers in a small discussion group. Choose the best answers and role-play two of the situations.

1. Picnic on the beach or in the park _____

   _____

   _____

   _____

   _____

2. In a restaurant _____

   _____

   _____

   _____

   _____

3. At a high school party where there are no chaperones_____

   _____

   _____

   _____

   _____

4. At a fraternity party on a college campus_____

   _____

   _____

   _____

   _____

5. Riding around in a car _____

   _____

   _____

   _____

   _____

6. In a friend's home when parents are gone _____

   _____

   _____

   _____

   _____

# Drug Terms

**Activity G**

**Chapter 7**

Name _____

Date _____ Period _____

Match the following terms with their descriptive phrases.

_____ 1. Deliberately taking a substance for other than its intended purpose, and in a manner that can result in damage to the person's health or ability to function.

_____ 2. Dependence on a drug that occurs when the body chemistry of a user is altered by repeated use of a drug and the user develops an actual physical need for the drug.

_____ 3. Physical dependence on a drug when a person builds up a tolerance and must have increasing amounts in order to get the same effects.

_____ 4. Dependence on a drug that occurs when the user has learned to use the drug as a mental and emotional crutch.

_____ 5. Describes psychological dependence.

_____ 6. New illegal drugs that have slightly altered formulas, but they closely resemble other illegal drugs, such as cocaine or heroin.

_____ 7. Drugs that induce sleep or stupor and relieve pain, such as opium, heroin, morphine, and codeine.

_____ 8. Drugs that slow down the central nervous system, such as alcohol, barbiturates, and some tranquilizers.

_____ 9. Drugs that speed up the central nervous system, such as amphetamines, pep pills, methamphetamine (speed), and cocaine.

_____ 10. Mind-altering drugs, such as Ecstasy, lysergic acid diethylamide (LSD), peyote, STP, and phencyclidine hydrochloride (PCP), that cause users to behave as though they are "out of their minds."

_____ 11. A drug also known as pot, grass, mary jane, reefer, or weed, that is a product of the hemp plant, cannabis sativa.

_____ 12. A behavior exhibited by long-term pot smokers who neglect work and adopt a "drop-out" personality.

_____ 13. Substances that give off fumes that are sniffed for a quick high.

_____ 14. Synthetic testosterone-like drugs that have tissue-building properties.

_____ 15. Drugs that are used to treat or prevent illness and are available without a doctor's prescription.

_____ 16. Drugs that are available only with a doctor's prescription.

A. addiction

B. amotivational syndrome

C. anabolic steroids

D. depressants

E. designer drugs

F. drug abuse

G. habituation

H. hallucinogens

I. inhalants

J. marijuana

K. narcotics

L. over-the-counter drugs

M. physical dependence

N. prescription drugs

O. psychological dependence

P. stimulants

# The Use of Drugs

**Activity H**                                     Name _____

**Chapter 7**                                      Date _____ Period _____

1. Place the letters in the blanks to rank the following, indicating your answer to the following statement: "In my opinion, the most dangerous consequences of drug abuse are…"

   (A) Problems with the law. (B) Loss of ability to make responsible judgments. (C) Loud and boisterous actions. (D) Drowsy and lazy feelings. (E) Exaggerated emotions. (F) Loss of ability to drive safely. (G) Damage to physical health. (H) Possibility of becoming dependent on drugs. (I) Loss of parents' and adults' respect. (J) Loss of self-respect.

   Most dangerous _____

   _____

   _____

   _____

   _____

   _____

   _____

   _____

   _____

   _____ Least dangerous

2. Place the letters in the blanks to indicate what you think are the most common reasons for drug abuse.

   (A) Low self-esteem. (B) Influence of friends. (C) Relief from pressures. (D) Boredom. (E) Rebellion against authority. (F) Pleasurable feeling the drug gives. (G) Started smoking cigarettes, which led to drugs. (H) Unable to say no to friends.

   Most common reason _____

   _____

   _____

   _____

   _____

   _____

   _____

   _____ Least common reason

3. How do you think the drug problem in this country should be handled?

   _____

   _____

   _____

   _____

   _____

# Saying No to Drugs

**Activity I**

**Chapter 7**

Name _____

Date _____ Period _____

Read each of the statements below that are commonly used to persuade young people to try drugs. Write a response to each that would say no to drugs. Then compare your responses with those of other class members.

1. "If you don't try this, I won't be your friend anymore."

   Your response: _____

   _____

   _____

   _____

   _____

   _____

2. "Come on. Everybody else is doing drugs."

   Your response: _____

   _____

   _____

   _____

   _____

   _____

3. "If you really wanted to be 'in,' you would give it a try."

   Your response: _____

   _____

   _____

   _____

   _____

   _____

4. "Don't you want to try it and see what it's like?"

   Your response: _____

   _____

   _____

   _____

   _____

   _____

*(Continued)*

**Activity I** *(Continued)*      **Name** _____

5. "You just think you're better than everyone else."

Your response:_____

_____

_____

_____

_____

_____

6. "Come on. You'll spoil everyone else's fun if you don't try it."

Your response:_____

_____

_____

_____

_____

_____

_____

7. "Isn't it about time you grew up?"

Your response:_____

_____

_____

_____

_____

_____

_____

8. "If you try some, it will make you feel really good."

Your response:_____

_____

_____

_____

_____

_____

_____

# 8 Lifestyle Options and Consequences

## Lifestyles

Activity A

Chapter 8

Name _____

Date _____ Period _____

Read the following statements concerning various lifestyles and give your opinion in the space provided.

1. I believe single living would be more difficult for (Complete one sentence.)

   a woman because _____

   _____

   _____

   _____

   a man because _____

   _____

   _____

   _____

2. I believe the greatest problems for a single person would be (Number the following problems from 1 to 12, with 1 being the greatest problem.)

   _____ loneliness

   _____ inability to do all household chores

   _____ difficulty in achieving financial independence

   _____ missing the spouse/parent role

   _____ feeling uneasy with career contacts of the opposite sex

   _____ feeling inferior to married people

   _____ lack of parental approval

   _____ lack of peer approval

   _____ limited social contacts

   _____ stigmas associated with single people

   _____ lack of meaningful personal relationships

   _____ image of not being stable in career

*(Continued)*

**Activity A** (*Continued*)                                    **Name** _____

3. I think the main reason marriage is the most popular lifestyle in our society is _____

   _____

   _____

   _____

   _____

   _____

   _____

4. Which of the following statements do you believe?

   A.   All married couples who can have children should have children.

   B.   Married couples should be free to choose whether or not they want to have children.

   I agree with statement _____ because _____

   _____

   _____

   _____

   _____

5. I think the greatest problems for a couple cohabitating would be (Number the following problems from 1 to 9, with 1 being the greatest problem.)

   _____ lack of commitment between partners

   _____ lack of legal basis

   _____ lack of social support

   _____ lack of parental approval

   _____ lack of peer approval

   _____ being denied interspousal protection

   _____ financial restrictions (Social Security, insurance, tax, etc.)

   _____ child custody question if relationship ends

   _____ ownership of property questions if the relationship ends

6. Living together before marriage is a good way to test for compatibility. I (agree/disagree) with this statement because _____

   _____

   _____

   _____

   _____

# Premarital Pregnancy

**Activity B**

**Chapter 8**

Name _____

Date _____ Period _____

Using the decision-making process, evaluate the four alternatives available to an unmarried pregnant teen. List the pros and cons of each alternative. Then choose the one you consider to be the best alternative and explain the reasons for your choice.

Alternative: Keeping the baby, remaining single

Pros _____

_____

_____

_____

_____

Cons _____

_____

_____

_____

_____

Alternative: Marriage

Pros _____

_____

_____

_____

_____

Cons _____

_____

_____

_____

_____

*(Continued)*

**Activity B** *(Continued)*                    **Name** _____

Alternative: Adoption

   Pros _____

   _____

   _____

   _____

   _____

   Cons _____

   _____

   _____

   _____

   _____

Alternative: Ending a pregnancy

   Pros _____

   _____

   _____

   _____

   Cons _____

   _____

   _____

   _____

   _____

Based on your evaluation of the alternatives, which do you feel would be the best option?

_____

Why did you make this choice?

_____

_____

_____

_____

# A Look at the Adoption Options

**Activity C**

**Chapter 8**

Name _____

Date _____ Period _____

A single woman who is pregnant may wish to have her baby adopted by a couple who are unable to have children. There are two major choices she will have to make if she selects this alternative: agency adoption versus independent adoption and open adoption versus closed adoption. Answer the following questions regarding these options.

1. Research and describe an agency adoption. _____

_____

_____

_____

_____

_____

_____

_____

_____

_____

2. Research and describe an independent adoption. _____

_____

_____

_____

_____

_____

_____

_____

_____

_____

3. Which of these two options do you think a woman should select and why? _____

_____

_____

_____

_____

_____

_____

_____

*(Continued)*

**Activity C** *(Continued)*                          **Name** _____

4.  Research and describe an open adoption. _____

    _____

    _____

    _____

    _____

    _____

    _____

    _____

    _____

5.  Research and describe a closed adoption. _____

    _____

    _____

    _____

    _____

    _____

    _____

    _____

    _____

    _____

6.  Which of these two options do you think a woman should select and why?_____

    _____

    _____

    _____

    _____

    _____

    _____

    _____

    _____

# Sexually Transmitted Infections–Myths and Truths

**Activity D**

**Chapter 8**

Name _____

Date _____ Period _____

Read the following statements about sexually transmitted infections. Indicate if you think each statement is a myth or a truth by checking the appropriate column. Use the space provided to indicate why the statement is a myth or a truth.

|  | Myth | Truth |
|---|---|---|

1. Birth control pills prevent sexually transmitted infections from being contracted. _____ _____

_____

_____

_____

2. STIs can be avoided by abstaining from sexual intercourse. _____ _____

_____

_____

_____

3. Once you have had an STI, you are immune and will never get it again. _____ _____

_____

_____

_____

4. HIV can be spread through contact with certain body fluids, such as blood and semen. _____ _____

_____

_____

_____

5. If two people are free from STIs and have no sexual or other intimate contact with other partners, they are unlikely to contract an STI. _____ _____

_____

_____

_____

6. If the symptoms for an STI go away, prescribed medications can be discontinued. _____ _____

_____

_____

_____

# Lifestyles and Health

**Activity E**

**Chapter 8**

Name _____

Date _____ Period _____

Match each term with its description by writing the correct letter in the blank.

_____ 1. Illnesses spread by sexual contact.

_____ 2. The legal process through which a child's legal guardianship is transferred from his or her birthparents to others.

_____ 3. A condition caused by a virus that attacks the immune system of the body, creating a weakness to infections.

_____ 4. A sexually transmitted infection that can cause pelvic inflammatory disease (PID), which can lead to infertility.

_____ 5. A baby born to a mother infected with this STI may develop a blinding eye infection unless treated promptly.

_____ 6. A sore is the first symptom of this sexually transmitted infection.

_____ 7. The occurrence of seizures following preeclampsia.

_____ 8. A serious inflammation of the liver that is caused by a virus.

_____ 9. A virus that attacks the immune system of the body, creating a weakness to infections.

_____ 10. A condition involving fluid retention, swelling of the fingers and feet, and a sudden rise in blood pressure.

_____ 11. A sexually transmitted infection that has no cure and may stay in the body and flare up at irregular intervals.

_____ 12. A condition caused by lack of iron in the diet resulting in a low level of hemoglobin in the blood.

_____ 13. Small, large, flat or raised warts in the genital area caused by a virus and spread by sexual contact.

_____ 14. Also called "crabs," these tiny insects are found in the human genital area and cause itching.

_____ 15. The purposeful decision to refrain from sexual intercourse or other high-risk behaviors such as alcohol or drug use.

A. abstinence

B. Acquired Immune Deficiency Syndrome (AIDS)

C. adoption

D. anemia

E. chlamydia

F. eclampsia

G. genital herpes

H. gonorrhea

I. hepatitis B

J. human immunodeficiency virus (HIV)

K. human papillomavirus (HPV)

L. preeclampsia

M. pubic lice

N. sexually transmitted infections (STIs)

O. syphilis

# Just Say No

**Activity F**

**Chapter 8**

Name _____

Date _____ Period _____

The following statements are often used to persuade a dating partner to have premarital sex. Read each statement and write a response that would say no to sexual involvement. Compare your responses with those of your classmates.

1. "If you loved me, you would prove it."

   Your response: _____

   _____

   _____

   _____

   _____

2. "We love each other so that makes it all right."

   Your response: _____

   _____

   _____

   _____

   _____

3. "If you don't love me completely, I'll find someone who will."

   Your response: _____

   _____

   _____

   _____

   _____

4. "We're not doing anything that all our friends aren't already doing."

   Your response: _____

   _____

   _____

   _____

   _____

5. "You've gotten me all excited! You can't tell me to stop now!"

   Your response: _____

   _____

   _____

   _____

   _____

*(Continued)*

**Activity F** *(Continued)*                                   **Name** _____

6. "Just relax. I'll know when to stop."

   Your response:_____

   _____

   _____

   _____

   _____

7. "Come on. You'll feel so good, I promise you."

   Your response:_____

   _____

   _____

   _____

   _____

8. "Nothing will happen the first time, so don't worry about it."

   Your response:_____

   _____

   _____

   _____

   _____

# 9 Communicating with Others

## Communication Survey

**Activity A**

**Chapter 9**

Name _____

Date _____ Period _____

Survey five people in your school about communication patterns in your school environment. Use the survey on the next page. Record the answers in the chart below. Compile the results of all class members and write a story for the school paper.

### Survey Responses

|  | Person 1 | Person 2 | Person 3 | Person 4 | Person 5 |
|---|---|---|---|---|---|
| Indicate person's grade level or position, such as teacher, counselor, etc. |  |  |  |  |  |
| Question 1. |  |  |  |  |  |
| 2. |  |  |  |  |  |
| 3. |  |  |  |  |  |
| 4. |  |  |  |  |  |
| 5. |  |  |  |  |  |
| 6. |  |  |  |  |  |
| 7. |  |  |  |  |  |
| 8. |  |  |  |  |  |
| 9. |  |  |  |  |  |
| 10. |  |  |  |  |  |

*(Continued)*

**Activity A** *(Continued)*                    **Name**_____

## Communication in Our School

1. In general, I would say the communication in our school is _____.
   A. good
   B. fair
   C. poor

2. I think students show their friendliness by communicating to new students _____.
   A. often
   B. sometimes
   C. only when told to
   D. never

3. New students in our school _____.
   A. would feel very lost
   B. could make friends easily if they tried
   C. would have no problem making new friends

4. I think the student-to-student communication is _____.
   A. good
   B. fair
   C. poor

5. The communication between teachers and students is _____.
   A. open and warm
   B. cold and stilted
   C. somewhere in between

6. I think the communication between teachers and students could be improved by _____.
   A. teachers taking more time for personal conversations with students
   B. students seeking out teachers more often
   C. having formal time periods set aside for discussions between students and teachers

7. The communication between students and counselors is _____.
   A. open and warm
   B. cold and stilted
   C. somewhere in between

8. I think the communication between counselors and students could be improved by _____.
   A. students taking more time for personal conversations with counselors
   B. counselors taking more time for personal conversations with students
   C. having formal time periods set aside for discussions between students and counselors

9. The communication between students and administrators is _____.
   A. open and warm
   B. cold and stilted
   C. somewhere in between

10. I think the communication between administrators and students could be improved by _____.
    A. students taking more time for personal conversations with administrators
    B. administrators taking more time for personal conversations with students
    C. having formal time periods set aside for discussions between administrators and students

# Communication–Helping or Hindering?

**Activity B**

**Chapter 9**

Name _____

Date _____ Period _____

Classify the characteristics listed below into two columns to indicate whether they help or hinder communication.

Takes words out of context
Encourages talk
Smiles
Is bossy
Willing to listen
Never listens
Indifferent
Gloomy
Skeptical

Listens selectively
Nods head
Shows interest in what others have to say
Makes others feel good about themselves
Over sympathetic
Makes others feel guilty
Gives in all the time

Gives feedback
Cheerful
Explains reasons for doing things
Belittles what is said
Optimistic
Sarcastic
Dominating
Makes eye contact

**Characteristics that help communication:**

_____
_____
_____
_____
_____
_____
_____
_____
_____
_____
_____

**Characteristics that hinder communication:**

out of context
bossy
not listening
indiff.
gloomy
skeptical

Explain how using some of the helpful characteristics could solve a communication problem.

_____
_____
_____
_____
_____
_____
_____

# Sympathy vs. Empathy

**Activity C**

Name _____

**Chapter 9**

Date _____ Period _____

Put an **S** in the blank in front of the statements that show sympathy. Put an **E** in the blank in front of the statements that show empathy. Add three empathetic statements and explain why empathy is more likely to be appreciated than sympathy.

_____ 1. "I'm feeling horrible because you're so sick."

_____ 2. "I realize how tired you must feel, so let's stay home and watch television."

_____ 3. "I'm so upset that you've had such a frustrating time."

_____ 4. "I know how you feel because I went through that very thing when I was working there."

_____ 5. "I understand why you feel that way, so don't say any more."

_____ 6. "I'm upset and feel just as bad as you do since I heard the news."

_____ 7. "I know you have had a rough time, and I'll accept your feelings, but I have to continue with the plan."

_____ 8. _____

_____

_____

_____ 9. _____

_____

_____

_____ 10. _____

_____

_____

Empathy is more likely to be appreciated than sympathy because _____

_____

_____

_____

_____

# Communication Checklist

**Activity D**

**Chapter 9**

Name _____

Date _____ Period _____

The following communication practices promote good relations with others. Evaluate your communication skills by responding to each of the following statements according to the way it describes you. Mark **A** for always, **S** for sometimes, and **N** for never. Then score your response by following the directions below.

_____ 1. I seek out a person's interests and ask questions the other person likes to answer.

_____ 2. I try to choose a time and place that's good for communication.

_____ 3. I let my friends know how important their friendship is to me.

_____ 4. I often compliment my friends.

_____ 5. When I must discuss a difficult subject with someone, I rehearse what I want to say in order to avoid hurt feelings.

_____ 6. I tune out self-defeating messages and focus on positive thoughts that encourage communication.

_____ 7. I am confident in stating my opinions even if they differ from those of others'.

_____ 8. I respect the right of others to have differing opinions.

_____ 9. I do not get upset when someone disagrees with something I have said.

_____ 10. I listen closely to what others have to say.

_____ 11. My friends trust me completely.

_____ 12. Others know they can count on me when they need help.

_____ 13. I am optimistic and always try to see the bright side.

_____ 14. I listen with an open mind and avoid hasty judgments.

_____ 15. I am patient enough to tolerate situations that are less than ideal and wait for better times.

_____ 16. I project a positive image when people meet me for the first time.

_____ 17. I keep my hair, hands, and fingernails clean and well groomed.

_____ 18. I wear clean clothing that is appropriate for the occasion.

_____ 19. My hand gestures aid communication rather than distract.

_____ 20. I maintain eye contact when talking with others.

_____ 21. I know and practice proper etiquette.

_____ 22. I am able to say no without feeling guilty or apologetic.

_____ 23. I stand up for my own beliefs without attacking the beliefs of others.

_____ 24. I express myself without putting others down.

_____ 25. I can admit anger and express it without resorting to physical or verbal abuse.

Give yourself two points for each response marked **A** and one point for each response marked **S**. Add up your total points. If you scored 36 or more, your communication skills have led you to have many close friends; 31–35, you probably have many friends; 26–30, you have good communication skills; 25 or less, you might want to review your communication practices in order to encourage closer relations with others.

_____ **A** responses × 2 = _____

_____ **S** responses × 1 = + _____

Score _____

# Family Communication

**Activity E**                                    Name _____

**Chapter 9**                                    Date _____ Period _____

The following are some of the suggestions your text listed for improving family communication. During the next three days, try to use each of these suggestions at least once. Briefly describe the situation where you used each suggestion. Tell how you used the technique and then evaluate how effective the technique was in aiding communication. Answer the remaining questions.

1. Pick a good time to begin discussing a problem. Choose a time when everyone is relaxed and not pressed for time.

   Describe the situation: _____

   _____

   _____

   How did you use the technique? _____

   _____

   _____

   _____

   How effective was this technique in aiding communication? _____

   _____

   _____

2. Indicate your honest wish to talk. Parents may not be aware that you want to talk.

   Describe the situation: _____

   _____

   _____

   How did you use the technique? _____

   _____

   _____

   How effective was this technique in aiding communication? _____

   _____

   _____

   _____

3. Retain a pleasant tone of voice and avoid critical or sarcastic remarks.

   Describe the situation: _____

   _____

   _____

   How did you use the technique? _____

   _____

   _____

*(Continued)*

**Activity E** *(Continued)* Name _____

How effective was this technique in aiding communication? _____

_____

_____

_____

4. Use I-messages rather than you-messages to express how you feel without criticizing or blaming others.

Describe the situation: _____

_____

_____

How did you use the technique? _____

_____

_____

_____

How effective was this technique in aiding communication? _____

_____

_____

_____

5. Know when to give up a lost cause and end an argument. You cannot expect to get your way all the time.

Describe the situation: _____

_____

_____

How did you use the technique? _____

_____

_____

_____

How effective was this technique for aiding communication? _____

_____

_____

_____

6. Suggest dropping the issue for the time being, allowing each person to calm down and think rationally.

Describe the situation: _____

_____

_____

*(Continued)*

**Activity E** *(Continued)*        **Name** _____

How did you use the technique? _____

_____

_____

_____

How effective was this technique in aiding communication? _____

_____

_____

_____

7. Which technique did you feel was the most effective in improving family communication? Why?

_____

_____

_____

_____

_____

_____

8. Which technique did you feel was the least effective in improving family communication? Why?

_____

_____

_____

_____

_____

_____

9. What have you learned about improving family communication?

_____

_____

_____

_____

_____

_____

_____

# 10 Communication Challenges

## Overcoming Prejudices

Name _____

Date _____ Period _____

Read the following case studies. Then write your answers to the questions. Be prepared to discuss your conclusions in class.

1. Lan, an eighteen-year-old Asian female, was anxious to be able to vote in her first election. Lan's parents were very involved in their political party and often talked to Lan about politics. Lan developed strong political views that were similar to her parents'. She then began asking her friends how they intended to vote in the upcoming election. Lan became very angry with her friend Ashley and thought she was "stupid" because of the opposing political views she expressed. Lan refused to speak to Ashley anymore or return any of her calls.

   What is the cause of Lan's prejudice? _____

   _____

   _____

   _____

   How could Lan overcome her prejudice? _____

   _____

   _____

2. Jamal, a 16-year-old African-American male, had to complete his junior year at a school in another state so his father could start a new job. Jamal was shocked at the response he received upon arriving at the school. All of the students in his homeroom asked if he would be joining the basketball team because of his race. Students commented about how often the "really good" basketball players on television were always African-American. Jamal felt angry at this assumption. He did not even like basketball. Jamal enjoyed debate at his former school and he intended to join the debate team at his new school.

   How should Jamal respond to his classmates? _____

   _____

   _____

   _____

   How can Jamal's classmates overcome their prejudice? _____

   _____

   _____

   _____

# Sexual Harassment

**Activity B**                                Name _____

**Chapter 10**                               Date _____ Period _____

Read each situation below and write your answers to the questions in the space provided.

1. Every time Rita, a new young staff member, walks by Bill's desk, he grins at his male coworker in the adjacent cubicle and makes a remark about how attractive her body is. This makes her feel uncomfortable. She frowns and looks away, but the remarks are continuing.

   Is Rita experiencing sexual harassment?_____

   How should she deal with this situation? _____

   _____

   _____

   _____

   _____

   _____

   _____

2. Nick, a young man who is a temporary office worker, has a long-term assignment in an office managed by Val. Last week, when Nick stopped by Val's office to drop off some papers, she called him into her office and asked him to turn around slowly so she and her female colleagues could admire his attractive body.

   Did Nick experience sexual harassment? _____

   How should he deal with this situation? _____

   _____

   _____

   _____

   _____

   _____

   _____

3. Gretchen, an attractive older woman, enjoys her job at the design firm. However, every week for the past year, Oscar, a designer employed as a freelancer of the company, stops in her office and says, "You look terrific" as he puts his arm around her waist. Gretchen has asked Oscar repeatedly not to touch her. The next week, the same thing happens again.

   Is Gretchen experiencing sexual harassment? _____

   How should she deal with Oscar's unwanted attention? _____

   _____

   _____

   _____

   _____

   _____

   _____

# Valuing Diversity

| | |
|---|---|
| **Activity C** | **Name** _____ |
| **Chapter 10** | **Date** _____ **Period** _____ |

Complete the statements below, and be prepared to discuss your answers.

1. I would like to know more about the _____ culture in America because

_____

_____

_____

_____

2. I am descended from _____ culture.

This culture's most important contributions to America have been in the areas of_____

_____

_____

_____

_____

3. A historical figure from another culture whom I admire is _____.

I admire this person because _____

_____

_____

_____

_____

_____

4. My favorite food from another culture is _____.

5. If I could be fluent in another language, it would be _____

because_____

_____

6. The city or country I would most like to visit is _____ _____

because_____

_____

_____

_____

*(Continued)*

**Activity C** *(Continued)*                    Name_____

7. The American historical figure whom I most admire is _____,

   whose family originally came from _____.

   I most admire this person because_____

   _____

   _____

   _____

   _____

   _____

   _____

8. My favorite foreign actress or musician is _____.

9. My favorite foreign car is _____.

10. If I had to name a foreign country that has contributed the most to American culture, I would say

    that it is _____

    because_____

    _____

    _____

    _____

    _____

    _____

11. Cultural diversity should be valued because_____

    _____

    _____

    _____

    _____

    _____

    _____

    _____

    _____

    _____

# 11 Developing Close Relationships

## Dating Survey

Activity A

Chapter 11

Name _____

Date _____ Period _____

Survey five students in your school about their dating practices. Use the survey questions on the next page. Record the answers in the chart below. Compile the results of all class members and write a story for the school paper.

### Survey Responses

| Question | Person 1 | Person 2 | Person 3 | Person 4 | Person 5 |
|---|---|---|---|---|---|
| 1. | | | | | |
| 2. | | | | | |
| 3. | | | | | |
| 4. | | | | | |
| 5. | | | | | |
| 6. | | | | | |
| 7. | | | | | |
| 8. | | | | | |
| 9. | | | | | |
| 10. | | | | | |
| 11. | | | | | |
| 12. | | | | | |
| 13. | | | | | |
| 14. | | | | | |
| 15. | | | | | |

*(Continued)*

**Activity A** *(Continued)*                     Name _____

## Dating Survey

1. Your sex:
   A. Male.
   B. Female.

2. Your age: _____

3. Have you ever dated?
   A. Yes.
   B. No. (If no, answer only questions 6-11.)

4. If so, at what age did you begin dating? _____

5. Are you presently dating:
   A. no one
   B. one person
   C. more than one person

6. Which would you prefer?
   A. Going out on dates.
   B. Going out with a group of friends.

7. What would you like to do most on a date?
   A. Go to a movie.
   B. Go to the park or beach.
   C. Go to a school event.
   D. Go to a party.
   E. Watch a sports event.
   F. Go to a concert.
   G. Go out to dinner.
   H. Participate in a sport.
   I. Go to a religious function.

8. What is the most important aspect of a dating partner?
   A. Physical appearance.
   B. Popularity.
   C. Personality.
   D. Common interests.

9. Do you have a curfew?
   A. Yes.
   B. No. (If no, go to question 12.)

10. If so, when do you have to be home on weeknights? _____

11. When do you have to be home on weekends? _____

12. Do you prefer to:
    A. be alone with your date
    B. double-date
    C. attend a group function

13. What method of transportation do you usually use on dates?
    A. Own car.
    B. Family car.
    C. Public transportation.
    D. Bicycles.
    E. Ride with friends.

14. How much do you spend on an average date?
    A. Nothing.
    B. $10.00.
    C. $20.00.
    D. $30.00.
    E. $40.00.
    F. Over $40.00.

15. Where do you most often meet the people you date?
    A. Classes at school.
    B. School functions.
    C. Club meetings.
    D. Work.
    E. Religious function.

# Positive and Negative Types of Love

**Activity B**

**Chapter 11**

Name _____

Date _____ Period _____

Put a + in front of the statements that describe positive love. Put a – in front of the statements that describe negative love. Add five statements that describe love relationships in today's society. Indicate whether they describe positive or negative love.

_____ 1. You want your partner to fully develop his or her potential.

_____ 2. You accept your partner's faults and weaknesses.

_____ 3. You show the emotion of jealousy toward the person you love.

_____ 4. Receiving personal gratification is your primary objective.

_____ 5. You have each other's interests at heart.

_____ 6. Your love withstands the test of time.

_____ 7. Mutual respect and understanding are found in this love.

_____ 8. The love that raises its voice in anger against the loved one.

_____ 9. Your love is not returned, and you live in the agony of unfulfilled love.

_____ 10. Both of you feel happy, secure, and satisfied.

_____ 11. _____

_____

_____

_____ 12. _____

_____

_____

_____ 13. _____

_____

_____

_____ 14. _____

_____

_____

_____ 15. _____

_____

_____

# Love Match

Activity C

Chapter 11

Name _____

Date _____ Period _____

Match the following terms and definitions.

_____ 1. Hasty and changeable attraction to someone.

_____ 2. Love that raises its voice in anger toward the beloved.

_____ 3. Possessive love.

_____ 4. Unfulfilled love.

_____ 5. Vigorous, insistent form of love.

_____ 6. Tendency to hate people you love.

_____ 7. Love that involves total communication and commitment.

_____ 8. Love that is warm, secure, and cheerful.

_____ 9. One method of communicating deep feelings of affection.

_____ 10. Love based on mutual respect and understanding.

A.  ambivalence

B.  friendly

C.  hostile

D.  infatuation

E.  jealous

F.  passionate

G.  physical expressions

H.  tender

I.  true

J.  unreturned

# Communicating Affection

**Activity D**

**Chapter 11**

Name _____

Date _____ Period _____

Write your reactions to the following situations. Then share your ideas in a small group. Write a solution to each situation, combining the best ideas of the group's members.

"Bob and I dated all during our senior year at school. This fall, we are going to different colleges. We feel very strongly about each other and hope we will get married someday. We have handled our emotions cautiously, but it is getting harder as fall comes closer and closer. I have talked to friends, and they all say we should go ahead and have sexual relations. I feel our love is much deeper than anything physical and that we do not have to prove anything to each other. However, I really do love Bob. What should I do?"

Your reaction: _____

_____

_____

_____

Group's solution: _____

_____

_____

_____

_____

_____

"I've dated a lot of girls, but was never very serious about any particular one. Now I feel pressure from the guys to get really involved with a girl, and the girls add pressure, too. There is one girl in particular who I really like, but I don't want to get involved yet. How can I show real interest in her and yet let her know I don't want any sexual involvement?"

Your reaction: _____

_____

_____

_____

Group's solution: _____

_____

_____

_____

_____

_____

# Your Attitudes About Sexual Behavior

**Activity E**

**Chapter 11**

Name _____

Date _____ Period _____

Respond to each of the following statements by circling whether you agree or disagree. Then explain why you answered as you did.

1. I believe the responsibility for controlling sexual behavior lies with both the boy and the girl.

   I (agree, disagree) because_____

   _____

   _____

   _____

2. I believe the best way to prevent sexual involvement is to provide young people with the factual knowledge necessary for them to make appropriate decisions.

   I (agree, disagree) because_____

   _____

   _____

   _____

3. I believe parents, schools, and religious leaders should provide guidelines for young people concerning sexual behavior. The ultimate decision, however, rests with the individual.

   I (agree, disagree) because_____

   _____

   _____

   _____

4. I believe teens get mixed messages about sexuality from the media and from parents and other authority figures.

   I (agree, disagree) because_____

   _____

   _____

   _____

5. I believe some teens feel parenting a child is the best way to affirm their adulthood.

   I (agree, disagree) because_____

   _____

   _____

   _____

# Acquaintance/Date Rape

**Activity F**

**Chapter 11**

Name _____

Date _____ Period _____

Teens need to become more aware of the attitudes and situations that can lead to acquaintance rape. They need to develop prevention strategies to use if needed. Your text described several ways to protect yourself. Answer the following questions to personalize these strategies for your use. Share and compare your responses with your classmates.

## Prevention Strategies

1. **Respect the limits set by your parents or those in authority.**
   List family ground rules you think would be helpful to young people. Your list should include good age limits for group dating, single dating, and steady dating; curfews you feel young people should have for weeknights and weekends; guidelines for going to parties; and any other family rules that could help young people.

   _____

   _____

   _____

   _____

   _____

   _____

   _____

2. **Before you get involved in a difficult situation, you need to set your own personal limits.**
   What questions must young people answer for themselves in order to establish their own personal limits? List below.

   _____

   _____

   _____

   _____

   _____

3. **Learn how to recognize trouble situations and be alert to circumstances that might get out of control.**
   Describe what is meant by a situation that is getting out of control. What are the signs to watch for on a date? at a party?

   _____

   _____

   _____

   _____

   _____

   _____

*(Continued)*

**Activity F** *(Continued)*                                    **Name** _____

4. **Maintain your options for leaving a situation that is getting out of control.**
   What arrangements can you make ahead of time to allow for this option?

   _____

   _____

   _____

   _____

   _____

5. **Learn how to say no and mean it.**
   How would you respond in the following situations in order to avoid sexual intimacy? What would you say? What action would you take?

   A.  "You say you love me, but I want you to prove it."

   _____

   _____

   _____

   _____

   B.  "I just spent all this money on you. How can you say no?"

   _____

   _____

   _____

   _____

   C.  "Everyone else is doing it."

   _____

   _____

   _____

   _____

   D.  "If you don't make love to me, it's over for us."

   _____

   _____

   _____

   _____

   E.  "You can't get me all excited and then say no."

   _____

   _____

   _____

   _____

# 12 Engagement and Marriage

## Role Expectations in Marriage

**Activity A**

**Chapter 12**

Name _____

Date _____ Period _____

Complete the checklist indicating your opinions about role expectations in marriage.

**Agree   Disagree      I believe that:**

_____  _____   1. Women who graduate from college, marry, and become full-time homemakers waste their education.

_____  _____   2. More and more husbands seem willing to help with household duties and child-care responsibilities.

_____  _____   3. Ordinarily, the husband's position gives the family its status in the community.

_____  _____   4. Role expectations and practices are determined more by personal preference and desire than they are by cultural influence or socioeconomic status.

_____  _____   5. Husband and wife roles are no longer learned within the family structure.

_____  _____   6. The male's traditional role as head of the house has disappeared during the last century.

_____  _____   7. Even when a woman combines career and marriage, her role as mother and wife does not change to correspond to this.

_____  _____   8. If a wife has a successful career, she will usually damage her husband's pride.

_____  _____   9. In the future, more women will combine marriage with a career.

_____  _____   10. Decisions about who carries primary responsibility for household tasks should be decided according to gender.

Choose one of the above statements that you feel strongly about and write a response.

_____

_____

_____

_____

_____

_____

# Statements About Spouse Selection

**Activity B**                                Name _____

**Chapter 12**                             Date _____ Period _____

Write your reaction to each of the following statements. Then form small groups and compare ideas.

1. Individuals can change their partners' habits after marriage, so it does not really matter if they please each other completely before marriage. _____

_____

_____

2. There is really only one person in the world with whom you could be happy, so you must find that one person. _____

_____

_____

3. Parental approval or disapproval usually has no effect on a couple's relationship. _____

_____

_____

4. The proximity theory is not as valid today because of our technological society. _____

_____

_____

5. A good way to choose a marriage partner is to find a friend and let the friendship gradually develop into love. _____

_____

_____

6. When you find the right partner for marriage, you will know without a doubt that you are making the right decision. _____

_____

_____

7. It is better to seek out a marriage partner who is different from you in every way according to the theory of complementary needs. _____

_____

_____

# Career Goals in Marriage

**Activity C**

**Chapter 12**

Name _____

Date _____ Period _____

Complete the checklist indicating your opinions about balancing family obligations with career goals.

**Agree   Disagree**

_____   _____   1. A woman's only career after marriage should be in the home.

_____   _____   2. When you marry a person whose career involves the caring for and nurturing of others (such as a religious leader or doctor), you must accept that the person's first commitment may be to his or her career.

_____   _____   3. If one spouse's income is sufficient, the other spouse should stay home with the children rather than work outside the home.

_____   _____   4. If the career of your spouse involves frequent moving, you should be willing to do this without hesitation.

_____   _____   5. Once a woman has children, she should remain in the home and accept primary responsibility for raising the children.

_____   _____   6. A father may assist in the care of children without weakening his role as a man.

_____   _____   7. If one of the children becomes ill, the father should be just as willing to stay home from work and care for the child as the mother.

_____   _____   8. When both spouses work, the wife may be equally as committed or more committed to her career than her husband.

_____   _____   9. If a wife earns more than a husband, the husband will feel inferior and less important as a male.

_____   _____   10. If both spouses work, and both receive career-related invitations for the same evening, the man's invitation should take precedence.

_____   _____   11. Shift work is ideal for a working couple because it allows one parent to always be home with the children.

_____   _____   12. A spouse can influence the success of a career either positively or negatively.

_____   _____   13. If a wife is offered a good job in another state, the husband should be willing to move.

_____   _____   14. Good child care is easy to find for children if both the husband and wife want to work.

_____   _____   15. Child care provided by others is just as good as that provided by a parent.

I strongly (agree/disagree) with statement _____ because

_____

_____

_____

_____

_____

# Communication During Engagement

**Activity D**

**Chapter 12**

Name _____

Date _____ Period _____

The following topics may need to be discussed by a couple during the engagement period. Indicate how important you feel each topic is by checking the appropriate column. Compare your responses in class.

| Very Important | Somewhat Important | Not Important | |
|---|---|---|---|
| _____ | _____ | _____ | 1. Personality traits and habits you do not like in your future spouse. |
| _____ | _____ | _____ | 2. Educational goals you both may have. |
| _____ | _____ | _____ | 3. Career goals you both may wish to attain. |
| _____ | _____ | _____ | 4. Job demands of certain professions you or your spouse might choose. |
| _____ | _____ | _____ | 5. Who will handle the various housekeeping chores. |
| _____ | _____ | _____ | 6. Whether or not to have children. |
| _____ | _____ | _____ | 7. How many children to have. |
| _____ | _____ | _____ | 8. When to start a family. |
| _____ | _____ | _____ | 9. Will you or your spouse give up your job to take care of the children? for how long? |
| _____ | _____ | _____ | 10. Your sexual expectations, roles, and concerns. |
| _____ | _____ | _____ | 11. The type of wedding your families prefer. |
| _____ | _____ | _____ | 12. Spending habits and practices. |
| _____ | _____ | _____ | 13. Income sources and amounts. |
| _____ | _____ | _____ | 14. Monetary priorities and goals. |
| _____ | _____ | _____ | 15. A budget for the first months of marriage. |
| _____ | _____ | _____ | 16. Housing arrangements. |
| _____ | _____ | _____ | 17. Furniture preferences. |
| _____ | _____ | _____ | 18. Religious preferences and how to resolve any differences. |
| _____ | _____ | _____ | 19. Religious training of future children. |
| _____ | _____ | _____ | 20. Family planning concerns that may or may not be related to religion. |
| _____ | _____ | _____ | 21. The role of friends in your marriage (choice of friends, amount of time spent with friends, etc.). |
| _____ | _____ | _____ | 22. Health problems either may have. |
| _____ | _____ | _____ | 23. Hereditary problems that might affect children. |
| _____ | _____ | _____ | 24. Previous intimate relationships, if any. |

# The Engagement Period

**Activity E**

**Chapter 12**

Name _____

Date _____ Period _____

Couples should use the engagement period to identify any problems they may need to resolve before marriage. Many of these problems relate to career goals, education, personalities, religion, finances, friendships, and families. Read the following case histories of engaged couples and answer the questions.

**Brad and Carrie**

Carrie, 23, is engaged to Brad, 27. Carrie is studious, quiet, and friendly. A college senior, Carrie would like to continue her education and earn a master's degree. Her parents live in Arkansas. Brad is extremely outgoing and ambitious. He has completed his business degree and secured a high-paying job in Boston. He is from Boston, and his parents still live there. Neither Brad nor Carrie has brothers or sisters. They are both conservative. Brad is not religious, but his parents are Protestant. Carrie is Baptist. Carrie and Brad plan to rent a townhouse in Boston. Brad has lots of friends there, but Carrie is not always comfortable around them. Brad has been able to save some money. Carrie has a student loan to repay.

1. Describe the background of each of the partners. _____

    _____

    _____

2. Describe the anticipated strengths of each marriage. _____

    _____

    _____

3. What conflicts might arise in their marriage? _____

    _____

    _____

4. Should the couples marry as planned, or would you advise them to postpone, or even cancel, their marriage plans? _____

    _____

    _____

**Robert and Serena**

Robert, 20, is a foreman in a warehouse and Serena, 19, works as a clerk in an office supply store. They recently became engaged. Robert lives with good friends from his active social circle. Serena, who is much quieter, lives with her aunt and has few close friends. Both sets of parents live out of town. Robert has no savings and owes money on his car. He often runs short of cash before payday arrives. Serena, through careful budgeting, has managed to save a small amount of money. When she suggests to Robert that he should try to save more, he becomes angry. They plan to find an apartment close to Serena's aunt. They are both Catholic.

1. Describe the background of each of the partners. _____

    _____

    _____

*(Continued)*

**Activity E** *(Continued)* Name_____

2. Describe the anticipated strengths of each marriage. _____

_____

_____

3. What conflicts might arise in their marriage? _____

_____

_____

4. Should the couples marry as planned, or would you advise them to postpone, or even cancel, their marriage plans? _____

_____

_____

**Susan and George**

Susan, 32, is assertive, strong, and independent. She married when she was 17 and had a baby within a year. Her husband left her shortly after their daughter was born. She did not have any job skills, but she was able to work as a waitress while she earned an accounting degree. Eventually, Susan secured a good job and bought a townhouse. Although her monthly earnings disappear quickly, she has managed to stay out of debt. She has joined a Methodist church near her home. Her friends are mainly business associates. George has just asked Susan to marry him. He is 36 and lives with his parents. He has worked in his family's construction business all his life and has been able to save quite a bit of money. George, who is quiet and sometimes moody, is very close to his family and participates in Jewish customs and holidays.

1. Describe the background of each of the partners. _____

_____

_____

2. Describe the anticipated strengths of each marriage. _____

_____

_____

3. What conflicts might arise in their marriage? _____

_____

_____

4. Should the couples marry as planned, or would you advise them to postpone, or even cancel, their marriage plans? _____

_____

_____

# 13 Building a Marriage

## Making Marital Adjustments

Activity A

Chapter 13

Name _____

Date _____ Period _____

Your text lists five ways to make adjustments when disagreements arise in a marriage. Each of the five adjustment forms is used to resolve the disagreements described below. Identify the form being described by placing the following abbreviations in the blank preceding each one.

"CP" for Compromise
"AC" for Accommodation
"CC" for Concession
"M" for Martyrdom
"OH" for Ongoing Hostility

1. Amy wants to go to a very formal restaurant for dinner and David wants to go to a cafeteria.

    _____ A. Rather than argue, Amy goes along with David's choice.

    _____ B. Amy and David end up staying home and continue to argue all night.

    _____ C. David says he needs to talk with a business partner anyway and suggests he go to the cafeteria with him. Amy can then invite the partner's wife to go to the formal restaurant with her.

    _____ D. Instead of going to either place, Amy and David decide to go to a local family restaurant.

    _____ E. David agrees to go to the formal restaurant this time if Amy will agree to go to the cafeteria next week.

2. Sonja and Don received their tax refund check. Sonja wants to apply it toward a new TV, and Don wants to use it for a vacation.

    _____ A. Sonja will not give in to Don, and Don will not buy a new TV, so they put the money in a savings account.

    _____ B. Sonja and Don decide to keep the old TV, buy a DVD player, and rent DVDs describing vacation trips. Then they will pick the vacation destination they both like and save their money for a trip next year.

    _____ C. Sonja decides to go along with Don's plan for a vacation this year, but reminds him that next year they will do what she wants to do.

    _____ D. Sonja hates to start an argument so she says, "I really would rather have a TV we can enjoy all year, but I'll give in and do what you want to do."

    _____ E. Sonja and Don continue to find fault with each other's plans and they begin to argue about everything else as well.

*(Continued)*

**Activity A** (*Continued*)                               **Name** _____

3.  Jamal and Jennifer live in Illinois. Jennifer wants to visit her parents in Alabama and Jamal wants to visit his parents in Vermont on their two-week vacation.

_____    A.  Jennifer and Jamal plan a trip to Florida and invite both sets of parents to join them there.

_____    B.  Jennifer and Jamal continue to argue about vacation plans and they do not go either place all summer.

_____    C.  Jamal does not want to create a problem so he goes along with Jennifer's plan and complains the whole time about how they always do everything with Jennifer's parents.

_____    D.  Jamal and Jennifer decide to spend one week this summer with Jennifer's parents in Alabama and save one week to spend with Jamal's parents in Vermont in the winter.

_____    E.  Jamal and Jennifer cannot agree so he goes fishing in Canada and she goes to New York to shop and see shows.

4.  Melinda and James both work, and their small child becomes quite ill.

_____    A.  Melinda plans to work in the morning while James stays with their sick child. James will go to work in the afternoon when Melinda returns.

_____    B.  James says there is no way he can get time off from work right now because of inventory. Melinda uses a week of her sick leave, reminding James that he may have to do the caring another time.

_____    C.  James says he is just starting a new job and he cannot possibly take time off. Melinda is also at a crucial time in her career. She arranges to take their sick child to her mother's home, hoping the child will soon be better.

_____    D.  Melinda feels her job is just as important as her husband's, but she is always the one to make the sacrifice. She always ends up bringing her work home so she can stay with their child.

_____    E.  Melinda and James argue loudly, upsetting the sick child and causing the child to cry even more. Both are so upset the next morning they both feel sick and stay home from their jobs.

5.  Both Denise and Tom have interesting careers. Denise writes children's books and Tom is an engineering consultant. They live in a small home. Denise needs a lot of resources for her writing. She often has to use a lot of the space in their small home when she is meeting a book deadline. Tom is meticulous and organized and gets upset when his home is not orderly.

_____    A.  Tom gets upset one weekend when he cannot find some of his engineering proposals. He blames Denise for being so sloppy.

_____    B.  Tom realizes Denise has a deadline and offers to proofread her manuscript. They meet the deadline and together clean the house.

_____    C.  Tom lets Denise continue her writing to meet the deadline, but reminds her that next weekend his parents will be visiting. She will have to help him entertain them.

_____    D.  Tom says he cannot work in the messy house so he takes his work to the local library where he can concentrate.

_____    E.  Denise feels guilty that she is not fulfilling her duties. She puts her book aside and misses the deadline. She continues to remind Tom that she gave up her chance to publish a book so he could have a clean house.

# Conflict in Marriage

**Activity B**

**Chapter 13**

Name _____

Date _____ Period _____

Indicate whether you agree or disagree with the following statements. Discuss responses in class.

**Agree   Disagree**

_____ _____  1.  If two people love each other, they can handle all the problems of marriage.

_____ _____  2.  If there is something about your future spouse you do not like, you can always change him or her after you are married.

_____ _____  3.  After you marry, your feelings of love should remain at a constant level. If they do not, your marriage is in for trouble.

_____ _____  4.  If a couple never quarrel, they have a very good marriage.

_____ _____  5.  When a couple have their first conflict, it means their marriage is really headed for trouble.

_____ _____  6.  A marriage that has a lot of "loud" conflict is not as happy as a marriage that is fairly "quiet."

_____ _____  7.  In most conflict situations, each partner thinks the other partner is guilty or wrong.

_____ _____  8.  If both partners state the conflict as they see it, they may discover they have no real differing opinions and the problem was just misinterpretation.

_____ _____  9.  One partner should never say "I'm sorry," for this makes him or her appear to be the one who was wrong.

_____ _____  10.  Most couples quarrel with a "win/lose" attitude. The conflict ends with one partner winning and the other losing.

_____ _____  11.  Most conflicts can be turned into "win/win" situations. Both partners can win if they are willing to make compromises.

_____ _____  12.  Most authorities agree it is best to solve conflicts as soon as possible so they do not grow into larger problems.

_____ _____  13.  Sometimes more marital tension is created by trivial day-to-day problems than by major decisions.

_____ _____  14.  It is possible to have a "fair fight" in a marriage relationship.

_____ _____  15.  If a couple is having serious marital problems but only one spouse is willing to see a marriage counselor, there is no point in either spouse seeking counseling.

# Who Will Lead?

**Activity C**                                    Name _____

**Chapter 13**                                  Date _____ Period _____

Write your reactions to the following situations concerning leadership roles in marriage. Then discuss ideas in small groups.

1. Before they were married, Ron and Linda talked briefly about money management. Linda admired Ron's skill in handling financial matters. When they married, Ron announced he would take care of their money and simply give Linda money when she needed it. Two different shopping trips proved to be embarrassing for her because she had more groceries in her cart than money to cover the bill. She had to put some items back so she could pay the bill. She asked Ron to open a joint checking account at the bank so she could write checks too. Ron said, "I am the boss. I handle the money. You shouldn't try to buy more than you can spend." How can this problem be handled?

   _____

   _____

   _____

2. Carmen and Mario have been married for six years and have saved about $3,000. Mario announces he is going out to buy a boat. Carmen says they should keep the money in the bank so they can later buy a house. Mario tells her, "You handle the money for the groceries. I'll handle the money for big items." How can this problem be resolved?

   _____

   _____

   _____

3. Mary and Richard have been married for five years. They have two children, Melissa and Rickie. The children get along well most of the time, but they have some "squabbles" when they play together. Mary finds that shopping for groceries is easier when she goes to the store alone and Richard stays with the children. When she comes home, the children are often in tears. This is because whenever they begin to quarrel, Richard makes them sit in separate chairs and wait for Mary to come home and settle the argument. He tells Mary she is the boss when it comes to disciplining the children. Mary says they both have to discipline them. How can they settle this debate?

   _____

   _____

   _____

4. Becky and Bill have always enjoyed doing things together. They have joined bowling leagues, tennis clubs, and ski groups in order to enjoy recreational activities. Becky finds they get along fine if she allows Bill to take the lead role in these activities. Is this a good idea?

   _____

   _____

   _____

# 14 Family Life Today

## Family Roles and Responsibilities

Activity A

Chapter 14

Name _____

Date _____ Period _____

Many responsibilities must be carried out by various family members in performing the basic functions of a family. These responsibilities are often defined by a person's role in the family. In the appropriate spaces, list the various responsibilities that are performed in your family. Some examples are given for you. Then indicate whose role (mother, father, child, grandparent, etc.) includes each responsibility by placing the appropriate letter in the blank.

**M** Mother      **G** Grandparent

**F** Father      **O** Other relative

**C** Child

Some responsibilities may be performed by more than one family member.

| Responsibilities | Whose Role Is It? |
|---|---|
| Pays bills | M |
| Bathes children | F, M |
| | |
| | |
| | |
| | |
| | |
| | |

1. Who seems to have the most responsibilities in your family?_____

2. Do you think any adjustments should be made so responsibilities could be more evenly divided? Explain your answer. _____

_____

3. What could you do to help with more family responsibilities? _____

_____

_____

4. How would you alter these responsibilities in your future family?_____

_____

_____

# Identifying Family Structures

**Activity B**

**Chapter 14**

Name _____

Date _____ Period _____

Fill in the following chart. Cite examples of different family structures from movies, TV shows, literature, or history. Compare your chart with those of your classmates and discuss.

## Examples from Movies, TV, Literature, or History

| | |
|---|---|
| Nuclear Family | |
| Single-Parent Family | |
| Stepfamily | |
| Extended Family | |
| Childless Family | |
| Adoptive Family | |
| Foster Family | |

# Understanding Family Structures

**Activity C**

**Chapter 14**

Name _____

Date _____ Period _____

Several different types of family structures are discussed in your text. Describe each family system. In small groups, discuss some of the problems found in each system as well as the strengths of each. Then answer the remaining questions.

**Nuclear Family**

Description: _____

Problems: _____

_____

_____

Strengths: _____

_____

_____

**Single-Parent Family**

Description: _____

Problems: _____

_____

_____

Strengths: _____

_____

_____

**Stepfamily**

Description: _____

Problems: _____

_____

_____

Strengths: _____

_____

_____

*(Continued)*

**Activity C** *(Continued)*                                          Name _____

**Extended Family**

  Description: _____

  Problems: _____

  _____

  _____

  Strengths: _____

  _____

  _____

**Childless Family**

  Description: _____

  Problems: _____

  _____

  _____

  Strengths: _____

  _____

  _____

**Adoptive Family**

Description: _____

Problems: _____

  _____

  _____

Strengths: _____

  _____

  _____

How has the economy affected family structures? _____

_____

_____

_____

How does the role of children vary in the different family structures? _____

_____

_____

_____

# The Family Life Cycle

**Activity D**

**Chapter 14**

Name _____

Date _____ Period _____

Your text described the stages in the family life cycle. In the chart below, list the stages in the family life cycle. Then shade or color the years you project you will begin and end each stage in your life cycle. (If you choose not to parent, your life cycle will not include all stages.) Then answer the questions below.

## Time/Life Line

| Age | 15 | 20 | 25 | 30 | 35 | 40 | 45 | 50 | 55 | 60 | 65 | 70 | 75 | 80 | 85 | 90+ |
|---|---|---|---|---|---|---|---|---|---|---|---|---|---|---|---|---|
| Stages: | | | | | | | | | | | | | | | | |
| | | | | | | | | | | | | | | | | |
| | | | | | | | | | | | | | | | | |
| | | | | | | | | | | | | | | | | |
| | | | | | | | | | | | | | | | | |
| | | | | | | | | | | | | | | | | |

1. Did you project the first stage to begin before or after age 25? Explain your answer. _____

   _____

   _____

2. Do you think the decision to begin the second stage will be a more difficult choice than deciding

   to marry? _____

   Why?_____

   _____

   _____

3. Which stage of the life cycle do you think will be the most difficult? Explain your answer.

   _____

   _____

   _____

4. Which stage do you feel will be the most enjoyable? Explain your answer. _____

   _____

   _____

*(Continued)*

**Activity D** (Continued)                    **Name** _____

5. In which stage will changing roles be most difficult? Explain your answer. _____

_____

_____

_____

6. Did you anticipate the last stage might have more years than most other stages? What does this
mean to you? _____

_____

_____

_____

7. If a couple chose not to have children, how would their life cycle vary from the norm? _____

_____

_____

_____

8. If parenthood were postponed, how would this affect the remaining stages of the life cycle?

_____

_____

_____

9. How would having children as a teen affect the life cycle stages? _____

_____

_____

_____

10. How can you as a young adult prepare yourself to find satisfaction in the evolving life cycle stages?

_____

_____

_____

_____

# 15 The Parenting Decision

## Views on Parenthood

**Activity A**

**Chapter 15**

Name _____

Date _____ Period _____

Complete the checklist of statements concerning parenthood. Tabulate the answers of all class members and discuss.

**Agree   Disagree   Unsure**

_____ _____ _____   1. A married couple who love each other, want children, and can afford to have children do not have to plan a family, so they do not need to use birth control methods.

_____ _____ _____   2. Deciding to have a baby is harder for a couple than deciding to get married.

_____ _____ _____   3. Discipline means that children need to be punished if they do something wrong.

_____ _____ _____   4. Having a baby will change a bad marriage into a good marriage.

_____ _____ _____   5. The main task of the parent is to respond to the baby's physical needs because babies do not yet have emotional needs.

_____ _____ _____   6. If a husband and wife both want a child and believe the birth of a child will expand their love, having a child can be very rewarding.

_____ _____ _____   7. Men cannot enjoy handling a new baby because they are unsure of what to do with the baby.

_____ _____ _____   8. The best philosophy concerning child-parent relationships is that children like to be "pals" with their parents.

_____ _____ _____   9. Having a baby is a privilege and should not be considered a duty.

_____ _____ _____   10. Every child has a right to be a wanted child. Thus, decisions about family planning should be made by the husband and wife together.

_____ _____ _____   11. It is always the responsibility of the wife to use birth control measures so pregnancies can be planned.

_____ _____ _____   12. Couples may become so involved with careers they postpone or even bypass parenthood.

_____ _____ _____   13. After a couple marries, they must decide whether or not to become parents.

_____ _____ _____   14. Once you have a child your parenting role will always affect, and be affected by, your career.

# Deciding About Parenthood

**Activity B**

**Chapter 15**

Name _____

Date _____ Period _____

If you want to be a parent, you have to ask yourself if you like children and enjoy being with them. Ask yourself the following questions concerning your desire to be a parent. Discuss your responses with other classmates in a small group.

**Yes      No      Unsure**

_____ _____ _____    1. I enjoy being with children.

_____ _____ _____    2. It is easy for me to talk to children.

_____ _____ _____    3. I like to play games with children.

_____ _____ _____    4. If I had to choose between having children and advancing in my career, I would choose having children.

_____ _____ _____    5. I do not think children would keep me from reaching my goals.

_____ _____ _____    6. I would be able to love my children even when they had done something wrong.

_____ _____ _____    7. I would be able to handle the responsibility of caring for my children all day and all night.

_____ _____ _____    8. I would be able to help children learn right from wrong.

_____ _____ _____    9. I would be willing to give up much of my social life to take on the responsibility of caring for my children.

_____ _____ _____   10. I would not be upset if my children needed me when I had planned to do something for myself.

_____ _____ _____   11. When I am with children, I do not let frustrating behaviors upset me.

_____ _____ _____   12. I would like to be called "mommy" or "daddy."

_____ _____ _____   13. I would be able to look upon each child as being unique and worthwhile.

_____ _____ _____   14. I would be able to control my anger in dealing with my children.

_____ _____ _____   15. I believe I could provide the financial support needed to raise a child.

_____ _____ _____   16. I would be able to give my spouse support if questions came up concerning the discipline of our children.

_____ _____ _____   17. I would seek professional help if I felt I had a problem dealing with my children that I could not resolve.

_____ _____ _____   18. I believe having children would add depth to the husband/wife relationship.

_____ _____ _____   19. If I was employed, I believe I would be able to balance my parenting role with my work role.

_____ _____ _____   20. I would be willing to read or take classes to learn how to be a good parent.

Based on how I answered these questions, I feel I (am/am not) ready to be a parent because

_____

_____

# The Human Reproductive System

**Activity C**

**Chapter 15**

Name_____

Date _____ Period _____

Match the following terms with the correct descriptive phrases.

## Male

_____ A. epididymis

_____ B. penis

_____ C. scrotum

_____ D. semen

_____ E. testes

_____ F. urethra

_____ G. vas deferens

1. External organ containing erectile tissue that fills with blood during sexual excitement.

2. Thick, milky fluid consisting of sperm and secretions of three sets of glands.

3. Oval organs in which sperm and the male sex hormone are produced.

4. Duct that extends through the penis and transports the sperm out of the body.

5. Structure in which sperm mature.

6. External skin pouches that contain the testes.

7. Long tubes that are attached to each epididymis and lead inside the body.

## Female

_____ A. cervix

_____ B. endometrium

_____ C. fallopian tube

_____ D. ovary

_____ E. uterus

_____ F. vagina

8. Organ where eggs are stored and matured and female hormones are produced.

9. Opening or neck of the uterus.

10. A mature egg passes through this organ on its way from an ovary to the uterus.

11. Pear-shaped organ that holds and nourishes the developing fetus.

12. The canal that becomes the birth canal at time of delivery.

13. Inner lining of the uterus.

# Methods of Preventing Pregnancy

**Activity D**

**Chapter 15**

Name _____

Date _____ Period _____

_____     1.   A device that is inserted into the uterus by a physician.

_____     2.   Shallow cup of soft rubber that fits over the cervix.

_____     3.   Method based on abstinence when ovulation is likely.

_____     4.   A small, thimble-shaped barrier that covers the cervix.

_____     5.   Sterilization for men.

_____     6.   An oral contraceptive that prevents ovulation by use of synthetic hormones.

_____     7.   Male contraceptive that fits over the erect penis.

_____     8.   Sterilization method for women.

_____     9.   Involves the careful observation of signs and symptoms of fertile and infertile periods.

_____    10.   Contains a chemical that immobilizes or kills sperm on contact. Available as creams, foams, or jellies.

_____    11.   The man removes his penis from the vagina before ejaculation.

_____    12.   A round, soft device that is inserted into the vagina to cover the cervix and prevent sperm from reaching the uterus.

# Diet During Pregnancy

**Activity E**

**Chapter 15**

Name _____

Date _____ Period _____

Plan a week's diet for a pregnant woman using the guidelines that follow.

## Basic Daily Diet for Pregnant Women

| Food Group | Recommended Amounts | Typical Servings | |
|---|---|---|---|
| Grains | 6 to 10 ounce equivalents | 1 slice bread<br>1 biscuit, muffin, or roll<br>1 cup ready-to-eat cereal<br>½ cup cooked cereal, grits, rice, or pasta | |
| Vegetable | 2½ to 3 cups | 1 cup vegetable, cooked or chopped raw<br>2 cups of raw, leafy vegetables<br>1 cup vegetable juice | |
| Fruit | 2 cups | 1 cup fruit<br>1 cup juice<br>½ large grapefruit<br>1 medium fruit (apple, orange, banana)<br>½ cup chopped, cooked, dried, or canned fruit | |
| Milk | 3 to 4 cups | 1 cup whole or fat-free milk<br>To equal the calcium content of 1 cup of milk, it would take:<br>1 cup plain yogurt<br>1½ oz. cheddar cheese<br>2 oz. American processed cheese<br>2 cups cottage cheese<br>1½ cups ice cream | MILK |
| Meat and Beans | 6 to 9 ounce equivalents | 2-3 ounces of cooked, lean meat, poultry, or fish<br>The following count as 1 ounce of lean meat:<br>¼ cup cooked dry beans or tofu<br>1 egg<br>1 tablespoon peanut butter | |

*(Continued)*

**Activity E** *(Continued)*                    Name _____

| | Breakfast | Lunch | Dinner | Snacks |
|---|---|---|---|---|
| **Sunday** | | | | |
| **Monday** | | | | |
| **Tuesday** | | | | |
| **Wednesday** | | | | |
| **Thursday** | | | | |
| **Friday** | | | | |
| **Saturday** | | | | |

# Health Practices of the Mother-to-Be

**Activity F**

**Chapter 15**

Name _____

Date _____ Period _____

Group Members _____

The health practices of the mother-to-be can dramatically influence the health of the baby as well as the mother. The following substances, practices, or illnesses can affect the unborn child. Work in a small group to research one of the following topics. Prepare a report to share with the class.

| | |
|---|---|
| Alcohol | Malnourishment |
| Nonprescribed medications | Rubella |
| Illegal drugs | Rh factor |
| Smoking | Gonorrhea |
| Preeclampsia | Syphilis |
| Anemia | Herpes |
| Excessive weight gain | Chlamydia |
| Underweight | AIDS |
| Exposure to X-rays | |

Topic: _____

_____

_____

_____

Sources used: _____

_____

_____

_____

_____

_____

_____

_____

_____

_____

_____

_____

_____

_____

_____

_____

*(Continued)*

**Activity F** *(Continued)*                    **Name** _____

Group members: _____

_____

Report title: _____

Report: _____

_____

_____

_____

_____

_____

_____

_____

_____

_____

_____

_____

_____

_____

_____

_____

_____

_____

_____

_____

_____

_____

_____

_____

_____

_____

_____

# 16 A New Baby

## How Newborns Look and Act

Activity A

Chapter 16

Name _____

Date _____ Period _____

Write descriptive phrases at each point on the following diagram to indicate how babies look at birth.

hair _____

shape of head _____

neck _____

cheeks _____

chest _____

shoulders _____

skin _____

abdomen _____

body proportions _____

arms and legs _____

hands and feet _____

nose _____

chin _____

eyebrows _____

eyelashes _____

eye color _____

average weight _____

average length _____

bones _____

muscles _____

Babies are born with several reflexes. Match each reflex with the correct description.

_____ 1. Babinski reflex

_____ 2. grasp reflex

_____ 3. Moro reflex

_____ 4. rooting reflex

_____ 5. tonic neck reflex

A. Newborns close their hands tightly when their palms are touched.

B. Newborns extend their toes when the soles of their feet are touched.

C. When newborns are touched on one of their cheeks, they turn their heads in that direction and open their mouths.

D. When newborns are startled by a sudden movement, they spread their arms and legs apart and then bring them together again.

E. When babies lie on their backs, they turn their heads to one side. If they turn to the right, their right hands go out, and their left arms go up.

# Observation of an Infant

**Activity B**                                     Name _____

**Chapter 16**                                     Date _____ Period _____

Observe an infant (under one year of age) and find out the following information. (You may need to ask some questions of the infant's parents.) Compare your observations with those of other class members.

Infant's name _____ Age _____ (months) Sex _____

Length_____Weight _____

1.  Describe how the infant sleeps. Does the infant sleep through the night? _____
    _____

2.  Describe how the infant cries. Do the arms and legs fling out when the baby is crying? Does the crying stop when the infant is picked up? _____
    _____

3.  Does the infant's head need to be supported? Is the infant's head steady? _____
    _____

4.  Did you observe any reflex actions (rooting, grasp, Moro, tonic neck, or Babinski)? If so, describe them._____
    _____
    _____

5.  Does the infant roll over? If so, describe the action. _____
    _____

6.  Does the infant show excitement when someone interacts with him or her? Describe the infant's response. _____
    _____

7.  Does the infant seem able to focus his or her eyes on an object? _____
    _____

8.  Can the infant's eyes follow a moving object?_____
    _____

9.  Does the infant sit? _____ Is any help needed from others or can the infant sit on his or her own? _____
    _____

10. How long can the infant sit?_____

11. Does the infant crawl? If so, describe his or her movements. _____
    _____
    _____

12. Describe any other gross-motor development you observed in the infant, such as standing or taking a few steps. _____
    _____

13. Has the infant established a schedule for feeding? _____

# Interview a New Parent

**Activity C**

**Chapter 16**

Name _____

Date _____ Period _____

Interview a new parent or ask new parents to come to class to relate their experiences when they first became parents. Find out the answers to the following questions.

1. When you experienced the birth of your new son or daughter, what were your feelings? (excitement, relief, anticipation) _____

   What was the first question you asked? _____

   _____

   What was the first thing you said to your spouse? _____

   _____

2. Do you and your spouse feel a deepened sense of commitment to each other? _____

   _____

   To your new baby? _____

   _____

3. Do you view the change of roles from husband to father and wife to mother as expanding and fulfilling? _____

   _____

   Do you ever feel these new roles are more confining? _____

   _____

4. How did the birth of your baby affect your schedule? _____

   _____

   Who has the primary care of the baby? _____

   Who gets up during the night to care for the baby? _____

5. Have you had to change your lifestyle in order to stay home with your baby? _____ What changes have you made? _____

   _____

6. Do you feel your spouse should do more or less to care for the baby? _____

7. What are some of the worries you have concerning your new baby? _____

   _____

8. Do you feel you received adequate information on how to care for your newborn? _____

   _____

9. What advice would you give to new parents? _____

   _____

   _____

# Meeting a Newborn's Needs

**Activity D**                    Name _____

**Chapter 16**                    Date _____ Period _____

Newborns need sleep, food, and exercise. Complete the following sentences concerning the newborn's needs.

1. Newborns will sleep for about _____ to _____ hours a day.

2. Normally they have _____ feedings a day, or one every _____ hours.

3. At first, newborns will need to be fed during the _____, as well as during the day.

4. To help reduce the risk of SIDS, babies should be placed on their _____ to sleep in a crib. Babies should *not* be placed on their _____.

5. Mealtimes can satisfy _____ needs as well as physical ones.

6. The two types of diapers are _____ diapers and _____ diapers.

7. Choose clothes that are _____ so the baby can move freely.

8. _____ fabrics are the most desirable for the newborn's clothes because they are soft and absorbent.

9. Check the labels on baby clothes to make sure they have met the government regulations for _____.

10. Be careful not to _____ a baby, since babies warm up and cool off faster than adults.

11. When bathing or dressing a baby or changing the baby's diapers, the most important thing to remember is to *never*, under any circumstances, _____

   _____

12. When a baby cries, the baby may be trying to tell you one of the following four things:

   A. _____

   B. _____

   C. _____

   D. _____

13. Children grow and develop according to a patterned _____.

14. _____ is sometimes shown by babies when adults they love leave them for a short time, and the babies fear the adults will not return.

15. The newborn communicates by crying, and answering cries promptly does not _____ the baby.

16. Fear as an emotion begins around _____ months of age.

# 17 Helping Children Grow and Develop

## Keeping Children Safe

**Activity A**

**Chapter 17**

Name _____

Date _____ Period _____

Children need an environment that is safe. Parents need to be aware of hazards that exist in their homes. Listed below are safety hazards that can pose a danger to young children. Describe the danger each poses, then describe how you could eliminate or reduce the risk of each hazard.

| Safety Hazard | Danger Posed | How to Reduce the Risk |
|---|---|---|
| Poisons, cleaning agents, and medicines | | |
| Electrical outlets, cords, and small appliances | | |
| Stairs, railings, doors, and windows | | |
| Stoves, pots, and pans | | |
| Window-blind cords | | |
| Bathtubs and toilets | | |

# The Preschooler

**Activity B**

**Chapter 17**

Name _____

Date _____ Period _____

Interview a parent of a preschool child. Ask the following questions concerning the child's development and the parents' guidance techniques.

Age of child: _____

1. One way children learn is by imitating adults. This is called *modeling*. Can you give some examples of adult behaviors you have seen your child model or imitate? _____

   _____

   _____

2. How have you used the same guidance technique of positive reinforcement with your child? ____

   _____

   _____

3. What types of negative behavior does your child sometimes display? How do you handle such behaviors? _____

   _____

   _____

4. Have you observed your child in parallel play? Describe his or her behavior. _____

   _____

   _____

5. Have you observed your child in cooperative play? Describe an instance of cooperative play. ____

   _____

   _____

6. What are some limits you have set for your child's behavior? _____

   _____

7. Is consistency important in disciplining your child? _____

   _____

8. Do you use consequences when guiding your preschooler's behavior? _____

   _____

9. How do you use timeouts when guiding your preschooler's behavior? _____

   _____

   _____

10. Does your child have any specific fears? _____

    _____

    _____

# When You Were a Child

**Activity C**

**Chapter 17**

Name _____

Date _____ Period _____

1. Describe a time when you were disciplined as a child. _____

   _____

   What was your reaction then? _____

   _____

   What are your feelings now? _____

   _____

2. Describe a fear you had as a child. _____

   _____

   Tell how you overcame your fear. _____

   _____

3. Describe a time when you were angry as a child. _____

   _____

   How did others respond to your anger? _____

   _____

   How do you feel about the situation now? _____

   _____

4. Do you have a younger brother or sister? _____ Were you ever jealous of him or her? _____
   How would you prepare your child for a new brother or sister? _____

   _____

5. Did you have a friend your parents didn't like? _____ If so, what happened? _____

   _____

   Put yourself in your parents' place. What would you have done? _____

   _____

6. Relate a lie you told as a child. _____

   _____

   How would you react to your child's lies? _____

   _____

7. Were you ever given an allowance? _____ Were you ever paid for doing jobs at home? _____
   How would you teach your child money-management skills? _____

   _____

# Checklist for a Child Care Center

**Activity D**

**Chapter 17**

Name _____

Date _____ Period _____

Select a child care center to visit and observe. Use the checklist below to evaluate the quality of the facility. Total the number of checks marked in the **yes** column and compare your results with those of other class members.

Name of center visited: _____

| Yes | No | |
|-----|-----|---|
| _____ | _____ | 1. Is the center licensed? |
| _____ | _____ | 2. Is the center bright, colorful, cheerful, and child oriented? |
| _____ | _____ | 3. Is there an "isolation area" for ill children? |
| _____ | _____ | 4. Are emergency procedures and phone numbers clearly posted? |
| _____ | _____ | 5. Are the menus posted, and are the meals nutritious and appetizing? |
| _____ | _____ | 6. If there is an infant/toddler area, is it clean, well equipped, and properly staffed? |
| _____ | _____ | 7. Is there a quiet and comfortable place for naps? |
| _____ | _____ | 8. Does the outdoor play area have equipment that encourages active play and gross-motor development? |
| _____ | _____ | 9. Is there suitable indoor equipment for quiet individual play as well as creative small group play? |
| _____ | _____ | 10. Are parents welcome and encouraged to visit any time? |
| _____ | _____ | 11. Is the director a professional and competent person? |
| _____ | _____ | 12. Is the staff warm and loving, yet firm when necessary? |
| _____ | _____ | 13. Does the staff have training in child care methods and techniques? |
| _____ | _____ | 14. Does the staff respect each child as an individual and teach children to respect the rights of others? |
| _____ | _____ | 15. Does the staff seem to be sensitive to the needs and feelings of children and parents? |
| _____ | _____ | 16. Does the center emphasize parent communication and involvement? |
| _____ | _____ | 17. Is the staff enthusiastic about their responsibilities? |
| _____ | _____ | 18. Does the center have a written, planned program you can see being used? |
| _____ | _____ | 19. Are the children grouped according to age? |
| _____ | _____ | 20. Are the learning programs appropriate for each age group? |
| _____ | _____ | 21. Is the adult-child ratio acceptable? |
| _____ | _____ | 22. Is there appropriate nurturing and interaction with the infant/toddler-age child? |
| _____ | _____ | 23. Is the cost for each child reasonable? |
| _____ | _____ | 24. Is the discipline used appropriate without being harsh? |
| _____ | _____ | 25. Are the hours and days of operation flexible enough to meet the various working schedules of parents? |

# Evaluating Child Care

**Activity E**

**Chapter 17**

Name _____

Date _____ Period _____

Group members:_____

As a group, visit a local child care facility. Choose from the following types: family child care, nationally franchised child care center, privately owned child care center, child care linked to religious institutions, university-linked child care, publicly sponsored child care, cooperative child care, and employer-sponsored child care. Evaluate the following points at the facility you visit:

**Physical environment:** Is it attractive, clean, safe, roomy, and appropriate for children?
**Adult-child ratio:** How many children are supervised by each adult?
**Quality of program:** Are routines structured and educational activities planned?
**Staff interaction with children:** Is the staff trained in child care, and do they interact well with the children?

Each group will report their findings to the class. As each group reports, rate the quality of child care at each facility on the chart on the opposite page. Use the following rating scale:

Excellent ....... 4
Good ............ 3
Fair ............... 2
Poor .............. 1

Then answer the questions below.

1. Which child care facility did you rate as one of the best in your community?_____

   What were the best features about this facility? _____

   _____

   _____

2. If you were a parent seeking child care, which facility would you select? Explain your choice.

   _____

   _____

   _____

   _____

3. Many authorities feel a parent should be the primary caregiver for at least the first three years of life. Do you agree? Give your reasons. _____

   _____

   _____

   _____

   _____

*(Continued)*

**Activity E** *(Continued)*                                    **Name**_____

| Type of Child Care Facility | Physical Environment | Adult-Child Ratio | Quality of Program | Staff Interaction with Children | Other Comments | Totals |
|---|---|---|---|---|---|---|
|  |  |  |  |  |  |  |
|  |  |  |  |  |  |  |
|  |  |  |  |  |  |  |
|  |  |  |  |  |  |  |
|  |  |  |  |  |  |  |
|  |  |  |  |  |  |  |
|  |  |  |  |  |  |  |
|  |  |  |  |  |  |  |

# 18 Balancing Family and Work Concerns

## Blending Employment with Family Life

Activity A

Chapter 18

Name _____

Date _____ Period _____

Respond to the following statements concerning dual-career families. Use these statements as a basis for class discussion. (There are no right or wrong answers.)

**Agree   Disagree   Unsure**

_____ _____ _____  1. A woman's place is in the home, and she should be content being involved only with her home and family.

_____ _____ _____  2. A man's place is in the home, and he should be content being involved only with his home and family.

_____ _____ _____  3. The most fulfilling marriage is one in which husband and wife share household chores and childrearing responsibilities, and both have careers outside the home.

_____ _____ _____  4. Men and women today can choose if they want to be full-time homemakers or work outside the home.

_____ _____ _____  5. A mother can go back to work after a child is four weeks old without any adverse effects on the child.

_____ _____ _____  6. More businesses should provide flexible work schedules so parents can be home when their children are there.

_____ _____ _____  7. Working parents feel guilty about not spending enough time with their children.

_____ _____ _____  8. Working women still bear the primary responsibility for home and family matters.

_____ _____ _____  9. Job sharing (two workers fulfill one job by staggering work hours) allows working parents greater flexibility and should be offered by more companies.

_____ _____ _____  10. Businesses should provide child care centers in the workplace so parents can be closer to their children.

_____ _____ _____  11. Children of dual-career parents are more self-reliant, help more around the house, and have a better relationship with their parents.

_____ _____ _____  12. Children in dual-career families are more likely to have problems in school and get into trouble.

_____ _____ _____  13. Children are less affected by whether or not their mothers are employed than by how happy their mothers are with their life choices.

_____ _____ _____  14. In a dual-career family, if a husband's job requires the family to move, the wife should not hesitate to give up her job.

_____ _____ _____  15. If a woman's career requires her to move, the husband should be willing to relocate.

# Job Sharing

**Activity B**

**Chapter 18**

Name _____

Date _____ Period _____

Imagine you and a coworker have received your company's okay to share one full-time administrative assistant position. This will allow each of you to spend more time with your families. You are good at math and financial functions. Your job-sharing partner excels at writing and editing. You both have top-notch computer skills. Your coworker will work in the morning, and you will work in the afternoon.

The two of you must divide up your duties. You have volunteered to try to divide the duties in a way that is fair and takes advantage of the strengths of each worker. In front of each job function listed below, indicate the following:

    1 = You think you should be responsible for the task.
    2 = You think your coworker should do the task.
    3 = You both should do the task.

In a small group, compare your answers with those of other class members.

_____ Check e-mail for messages from supervisor and each other.

_____ Write, input, print out, proofread, and correct routine letters for supervisor's approval.

_____ Process reimbursement forms for staff travel expenses. (Total expenses, allocate to accounting categories, and forward to Accounting).

_____ On Friday afternoon, collect end-of-week time sheets from staff, check for completeness, and forward to Accounting.

_____ Write a first draft of the office operating budget for the coming fiscal year for your supervisor's approval.

_____ Order office supplies as needed.

_____ Answer and screen incoming telephone calls.

_____ Fax letters and other documents at the request of your supervisor.

_____ Research and write a first draft of an extensive report outlining the pros and cons of various types of proposed desktop publishing software.

_____ Leave an e-mail message alerting your partner about what happened while he or she was away, newly scheduled meetings, and other priority items.

_____ Attend Monday-morning staff meetings and take detailed notes for your partner.

_____ Greet office visitors and, at the request of supervisor, take them on brief tours of your company's office facility.

_____ Maintain office subscriptions to newspapers and various periodicals. Prepare subscription renewal checks to send to Accounting for payment.

_____ Supervise the student intern, whose hours are variable.

# Setting Priorities

**Activity C**

**Chapter 18**

Name _____

Date _____ Period _____

Imagine you are a working parent whose "to do" list for this weekend includes the items listed below. You know you cannot possibly get them all done, so you must set priorities. Rank your priorities as follows:

    1 = High priority—absolutely must do
    2 = Medium priority—should try to do
    3 = Low priority—nice to do, but can be postponed or not done at all

After you have made your rankings, compare them with those of other class members.

_____ Shop for groceries for coming week.

_____ Wash the windows.

_____ Finish a report the boss needs first thing on Monday morning. (Allow 2 hours for this.)

_____ Fill prescription for your 5-year-old's ear infection.

_____ Gather up loose change in your top dresser drawer and deposit the money at the bank.

_____ Watch a DVD you have been wanting to see.

_____ Make the beds.

_____ Work out on your new home exercise equipment.

_____ Call a friend you haven't seen for a while.

_____ Do the laundry for the coming week.

_____ Polish the copper areas on your stainless steel pots and pans with copper polish.

_____ Watch a football game on TV.

_____ Bake a cake for the PTA bake sale Sunday night.

_____ Get a haircut.

_____ Take your 16-year-old to the mall to shop for a prom dress.

_____ Take the car to a garage for a tune-up and oil change.

How can setting priorities benefit working parents?

_____

_____

_____

_____

_____

_____

_____

_____

# Challenges for Employed Couples

**Activity D**                                           Name _____

**Chapter 18**                                           Date _____ Period _____

Dual-career couples face many challenges, including finding adequate child care, finding time to spend with the family, handling financial concerns, living with the possibility of wide income differences between the spouses, finding "emotional energy" to support each other, and deciding who stays home with ill children. State what you feel is the greatest challenge facing an employed couple. Then discuss how you and your spouse could handle this challenge.

Challenge: _____

_____

_____

How you and your spouse could handle this challenge: _____

_____

_____

_____

_____

_____

_____

_____

_____

_____

_____

_____

_____

_____

_____

_____

_____

_____

_____

# 19 Dealing with Family Crises

## Dealing with Crisis

Activity A

Chapter 19

Name _____

Date _____ Period _____

Read the two lists of crises below. Then number each list, beginning with the most devastating crisis and ending with the least devastating crisis. Do the activity below. Discuss methods of meeting various crises in class.

### Crises of Young Adults

_____ Selecting a career for life
_____ Severe illness of a family member
_____ Breakup with a loved one
_____ Divorce of parents
_____ Death of a friend or parent
_____ Moving to a new community
_____ Mental illness of a family member
_____ Criminal attack (type: _____)
_____ Pregnancy outside of wedlock
_____ Child abuse
_____ Family member becomes disabled
_____ Marriage of divorced parent to new partner
_____ Choosing a college or training program
_____ Family member addicted to alcohol or other drugs
_____ Other: _____

### Crises of Marriages

_____ Divorce
_____ Unemployment
_____ Child abuse and neglect
_____ Family member with disabilities
_____ Death of spouse
_____ Death of a child
_____ Severe illness of a family member
_____ Infidelity of spouse
_____ Family member addicted to alcohol or other drugs
_____ Moving to a new community
_____ Spouse abuse
_____ Criminal attack (type: _____)
_____ Remarriage
_____ Mental illness of a family member
_____ Other: _____

Choose a crisis from the list above. Tell how people can use the following resources to help them deal with this crisis.

Crisis: _____

Mental resources: _____

_____

Physical health: _____

_____

Family relationships: _____

_____

Financial resources: _____

_____

Friends and community: _____

_____

# Family Crisis

**Activity B**                                    Name _____

**Chapter 19**                                    Date _____ Period _____

Read the statements below and write the missing terms in the space provided.

_____ 1.  Marital conflict often ends with the crisis of _____.

_____ 2.  The crisis of _____ may force people to reeducate or retrain
themselves for their occupations.

_____ 3.  Physical _____ is the infliction of physical injury upon a child.

_____ 4.  Emotional _____ is the failure to provide children with love and
affection.

_____ 5.  A(n) _____ is a person who suffers from compulsive, obsessive
drinking that is beyond the person's control.

_____ 6.  _____ children account for most of the missing children in this
country.

_____ 7.  Situation in which a person's loved ones speak truthfully, out of
love, to confront a person with details of problem behaviors in
order to convince the person to seek help.

_____ 8.  Establishments that offer food and housing for people who have
nowhere else to go.

_____ 9.  As the number of older adults increases and the number of adult
caregivers decreases, _____ abuse is occurring more often.

_____ 10. Sexual activity between persons who are closely related.

_____ 11. _____ that is left untreated is a primary factor in suicide.

_____ 12. A _____ gambler is someone who is unable to stop gambling
despite harmful consequences.

_____ 13. Some families may find frequent _____ as opportunities to learn
about different parts of the country, while other families resent the
stress caused.

_____ 14. Can provide an immediate source of information for a person
experiencing a crisis.

_____ 15. Money used to finance a gambler's debts.

_____ 16. Love conflicts, broken engagements, divorces, or the death of a
loved one drive some people to attempt _____.

_____ 17. Many missing children are _____ by noncustodial parents
following divorce settlements.

_____ 18. An adult is more likely to become a victim of _____ abuse if he or
she was abused as a child.

_____ 19. Someone who unknowingly acts in ways that contribute to an
addict's drug use.

_____ 20. A _____ occurs when sexual intercourse is forced on one person by
another.

# The Crisis of Alcoholism

**Activity C**

**Chapter 19**

Name _____

Date _____ Period _____

Group members:_____

Work in a small group to discuss your views of alcoholism. Combine ideas and write the group's reactions to three of the statements. Your group may agree or disagree with each statement.

1. Job stress and family problems are the most common causes of alcoholism.

2. If your spouse is an alcoholic, the best help you can give is to learn more about alcoholism and show your spouse continued love and understanding.

3. If a woman drinks heavily during pregnancy, the baby will be adversely affected.

4. If your spouse is an alcoholic, you should try to eliminate all alcohol from his or her environment.

5. Alcohol is the one and only cause of alcoholism.

6. There are few sources of help available for alcoholics. They have to solve their problems on their own.

7. Alcoholism is inherited. If a parent is an alcoholic, the adult child will probably be an alcoholic.

8. If your spouse is an alcoholic, you should try to hide the fact from his or her employer.

Group reaction to statement _____: _____

_____

_____

_____

_____

_____

Group reaction to statement _____: _____

_____

_____

_____

_____

_____

Group reaction to statement _____: _____

_____

_____

_____

_____

_____

# Teen Gambling

**Activity D**                                    Name _____

**Chapter 19**                                   Date _____ Period _____

Gambling often starts during the teen years. Is gambling a problem among your friends or at your school?
Answer the following questions to find out.

| Yes | No | Unsure | **Do you know people in your school who** |
|-----|-----|--------|--------------------------------------------|
| _____ | _____ | _____ | 1. gamble? |
| _____ | _____ | _____ | 2. gamble during school hours? |
| _____ | _____ | _____ | 3. have stayed away from school to gamble? |
| _____ | _____ | _____ | 4. participate in gambling activities such as poker, sports betting, or dice? |
| _____ | _____ | _____ | 5. have a lot of money from their gambling activities? |
| _____ | _____ | _____ | 6. get a lot of attention from classmates because they gamble? |
| _____ | _____ | _____ | 7. come late to school or class because they are gambling? |
| _____ | _____ | _____ | 8. feel that when they lose a bet, they must bet again to win back their losses? |
| _____ | _____ | _____ | 9. gamble with money they were supposed to use for other things, such as lunch, or clothing? |
| _____ | _____ | _____ | 10. borrow money in order to gamble? |
| _____ | _____ | _____ | 11. sell possessions to get money to gamble or pay a gambling debt? |
| _____ | _____ | _____ | 12. lie to family members about their gambling? |

Write your response to the following statement:

I (do/do not) feel gambling is a problem because _____

_____

_____

_____

_____

_____

_____

_____

_____

_____

_____

_____

_____

_____

_____

# Depression

**Activity E**

**Chapter 19**

Name _____

Date _____ Period _____

Read the following statements concerning depression. Place a check in the column that best describes your opinion. Use the statements as discussion topics in class. (There are no right or wrong answers.)

**Agree  Disagree  Unsure**

_____ _____ _____   1. A general feeling of hopelessness is a common symptom of depression.

_____ _____ _____   2. It is okay to feel depressed because depression is a normal human emotion.

_____ _____ _____   3. It is natural to feel depressed when you experience a loss.

_____ _____ _____   4. Youth is the happiest time of life.

_____ _____ _____   5. No one should feel guilty about feeling depressed.

_____ _____ _____   6. People can lessen the effects of depression if they eat nutritiously, learn to relax, get physical activity, and avoid stressful situations.

_____ _____ _____   7. Feeling lonely can create feelings of depression.

_____ _____ _____   8. Most people experience mood cycles—minor ups and downs during the day or week.

_____ _____ _____   9. Depression can be contagious. You can "take on" the feelings of depression from another person or situation.

_____ _____ _____ 10. Being depressed means you have a serious medical problem.

_____ _____ _____ 11. When you are depressed, you should concentrate on an activity you do well. This will help restore your feelings of confidence.

_____ _____ _____ 12. "Time heals all wounds."

Choose a statement from the checklist above. Explain why you strongly agree or strongly disagree with that statement.

I strongly (agree/disagree) with statement number _____ because_____

_____

_____

_____

_____

_____

_____

_____

_____

_____

_____

_____

# Teen Suicide

**Activity F**                                    Name _____

**Chapter 19**                                    Date _____ Period _____

Read the following statements about teen suicide. Indicate if you think each statement is a myth or a truth by checking the appropriate column. Use the space provided to indicate why the statement is a truth or a myth.

**Truth     Myth**

_____  _____   1. Young people who talk about suicide never attempt it.

_____

_____

_____  _____   2. Most suicides among teens represent an attempt to resolve conflict, escape unhappiness, or punish important people in their lives.

_____

_____

_____  _____   3. Over half of all teens think about suicide at some time.

_____

_____

_____  _____   4. Suicide happens without warning.

_____

_____

_____  _____   5. Suicidal people really want to die.

_____

_____

_____  _____   6. Suicide can occur in any family, regardless of its socioeconomic category.

_____

_____

_____  _____   7. Adolescent males are more likely to attempt suicide than females.

_____

_____

_____  _____   8. Adolescent suicide is a cry for help, not a desire to die.

_____

_____

_____  _____   9. Asking a person about any suicide plans will increase the risk of that person's actually attempting it.

_____

_____

*(Continued)*

**Activity F** *(Continued)*                    **Name** _____

**Truth      Myth**

_____  _____  10. Honestly talking with teens about suicide will put ideas into their heads.

_____

_____

_____  _____  11. Tension in the home is a contributing factor in teen suicide.

_____

_____

_____  _____  12. Drug abuse is a strong risk factor for suicide.

_____

_____

_____  _____  13. A personal crisis, such as the loss of a loved one or the breakup of a relationship, can cause some people to consider suicide.

_____

_____

_____  _____  14. Suicides are more common in homes that have one or more guns.

_____

_____

_____  _____  15. If people feel so desperate and alone that they begin to think about suicide, they need to get help.

_____

_____

# Missing Children

**Activity G**

**Chapter 19**

Name _____

Date _____ Period _____

Read the following statements about missing children. Indicate whether you agree or disagree with each statement by placing a check in the appropriate column. Discuss your responses in class.

**Agree   Disagree**

_____  _____  1. Children can be left alone in the car for a very short time.

_____  _____  2. It is not so much the stranger that should be feared, but the situation in which the child is placed.

_____  _____  3. Most often children are lured by people the children do not perceive to be dangerous.

_____  _____  4. Children should not give their real names, addresses, or phone numbers over the Internet, or arrange to meet people they speak to online.

_____  _____  5. Schools should notify parents immediately if a child does not report to school.

_____  _____  6. If children indicate they do not want to be with someone, there may be a reason. If they feel insecure, parents should listen to them.

_____  _____  7. Fingerprinting your child is one of the best ways to assure finding your child if he or she is ever missing.

_____  _____  8. Children should be taught to never tell anyone over the phone they are alone. They should also be taught never to open a door for anyone if they are alone.

_____  _____  9. Buying clothes with your child's name printed on them puts an abductor on a first-name basis with your child.

_____  _____  10. Divorced parents who abduct their children in custody battles account for only a small number of missing children.

_____  _____  11. People who have legitimate ways to contact kids, such as youth group leaders, may sometimes harm or abduct children. Parents should monitor the organizations and the adults who work with their children.

_____  _____  12. A child is most vulnerable when alone. Parents should not allow their child to be alone in any place.

Select a statement from above:

I strongly agree with statement _____ because _____

_____

_____

_____

_____

I strongly disagree with statement _____ because _____

_____

_____

_____

_____

# 20 Divorce and Remarriage

## Views on Divorce

**Activity A**

**Chapter 20**

Name _____

Date _____ Period _____

Complete the checklist of statements related to divorce. Divide into small groups to discuss your responses.

**Agree   Disagree   Unsure**

_____ _____ _____ 1. If two people are having marital problems, they will be able to solve their problems if they stay married and give themselves time.

_____ _____ _____ 2. Once people are married, they should not consider divorce.

_____ _____ _____ 3. If marriage partners have several disagreements, it means that sooner or later they will divorce.

_____ _____ _____ 4. In a divorce, there is always one guilty person and one innocent person.

_____ _____ _____ 5. If divorce laws were stricter, there would be fewer divorces and hence more happy marriages.

_____ _____ _____ 6. The misconception that when you marry you should be happy all the time has increased the incidence of divorce.

_____ _____ _____ 7. When you marry the person you love, you should be able to expect that person to make you happy. If the person does not make you happy, you should get a divorce.

_____ _____ _____ 8. If people were better informed about marriage, they would make better decisions concerning marriage. Thus, there would be fewer divorces.

_____ _____ _____ 9. If parents are having marital problems, they should stay together anyway for the sake of their children.

_____ _____ _____ 10. When a teen's parents divorce, the divorce always affects the teen's life adversely.

_____ _____ _____ 11. Divorce laws in all states should be uniform.

_____ _____ _____ 12. The mother should always be awarded custody of the children.

_____ _____ _____ 13. The only thing that really matters when you marry someone is that you love each other.

I strongly agree with statement _____ because _____

_____

_____

I strongly disagree with statement _____ because _____

_____

_____

# Divorce Issues

**Activity B**

**Chapter 20**

Name _____

Date _____ Period _____

Write your reaction to each of the following statements. Then form small groups and compare your views.

1. Fathers are filing for, and being granted, custody of children in an increasing number of divorce settlements.

   _____

   _____

   _____

   _____

2. Garnishment of wages (withholding a portion of a person's wages) is being legislated in an increasing number of states to force a parent, if necessary, to make child support payments.

   _____

   _____

   _____

   _____

3. Women who helped pay for their husband's education are being awarded a portion of their husband's salary following a divorce.

   _____

   _____

   _____

   _____

4. Parental kidnapping, in which one divorced parent kidnaps his or her child from the other parent, accounts for a large portion of missing children cases.

   _____

   _____

   _____

   _____

5. Divorce mediation is sometimes required by judges before a divorce is granted. This is an attempt to reduce the number of divorces in our country.

   _____

   _____

   _____

   _____

# Blending Families

**Activity C**

**Chapter 20**

Name _____

Date _____ Period _____

Divide into small groups and discuss the following situations. Be prepared to share your responses with the whole class.

**Situation A:** Bob and Angela married two months ago. Each has custody of children from previous marriages. Angela's sons, ages 7 and 9, hero-worshipped their father and are having trouble accepting Bob as their stepfather. When Bob tries to administer much-needed discipline, they scream, "We hate you! You're not our father!" What advice do you have for Bob? How can Angela help? Could counseling help?

_____

_____

_____

_____

_____

_____

**Situation B:** Manuel has always brought his children presents when he returns from out-of-town business trips. Since recently marrying Jan, Manuel has continued this practice but has not thought to bring presents for Jan's children, too. Now Jan's children feel left out. Should Jan ask Manuel to bring presents for all the children? Who should pay for the presents? Should Manuel apologize to Jan's children for leaving them out?

_____

_____

_____

_____

_____

_____

**Situation C:** Elton was delighted when Betsy, a quiet, kind woman who had been divorced for many years, accepted his proposal of marriage. At the wedding reception, however, Betsy's three college-age children informed him they wished Betsy had remarried their father instead of marrying Elton. Betsy says that since her divorce, the children have been obsessed with their parents remarrying even though neither parent wanted to reconcile. Since the wedding, the children have been rude and hostile to Elton. What can Elton do? How can Betsy help?

_____

_____

_____

_____

_____

*(Continued)*

**Activity C** *(Continued)*                                    **Name** _____

**Situation D:** Zeshaun, a divorced father of two sons, ages 16 and 17, and Davina, a divorced mother of two daughters, ages 4 and 6, have married. Zeshaun's two sons like to stay up late and play loud music. However, Davina's children need to be in bed by 8:00 p.m. in a quiet house. What new rules need to be put in place in this stepfamily? Who should inform the children of the new rules? Who should enforce the rules?

_____

_____

_____

_____

_____

_____

**Situation E:** Tammy's mother is an alcoholic who is wonderful when she is sober, but she is often abusive when she is not. A year ago, Tammy's father gained custody of Tammy and her brother as part of a divorce. A month ago, he married Gloria. Tammy wants to have a good relationship with Gloria and believes Gloria can help her grow up to be a successful adult. However, Tammy is reluctant to get close to Gloria because she feels to do so would be disloyal to her mother. Her mother, who had hoped to be given a second chance at the marriage, is very hostile toward Gloria and calls her names. How would you advise Tammy?

_____

_____

_____

_____

_____

_____

# 21 Growing Older

## How the Human Body Ages

**Activity A**

**Chapter 21**

Name _____

Date _____ Period _____

Fill in the blanks to describe typical changes that occur as the human body ages.

Maximum size and strength of body framework reached at about age _____

Skin _____

_____

_____

_____

Bones _____

_____

_____

_____

Heart _____

_____

_____

_____

Blood vessels _____

_____

_____

_____

Hearing _____

_____

_____

_____

Sight _____

_____

_____

_____

*(Continued)*

**Activity A** *(Continued)*                          **Name** _____

**Reproductive system:**

Women _____

_____

_____

_____

Men _____

_____

_____

_____

Weight _____

_____

_____

# Aging Brings Change

**Activity B**

**Chapter 21**

Name _____

Date _____ Period _____

At each stage of life, there are gains and there are losses. For example, aging people may lose some strength or physical vigor, but they may gain new leisure-time interests. In the areas listed below, list the changes that are likely to occur during the later years of life. Indicate those changes that are negative and those that can be positive by entering them in the appropriate boxes.

| Emotional Aspects | |
|---|---|
| Negative | Positive |
| | |

| Physical Aspects | |
|---|---|
| Negative | Positive |
| | |

| Financial Aspects | |
|---|---|
| Negative | Positive |
| | |

*(Continued)*

**Activity B** *(Continued)*                                    Name _____

| Housing | |
|---|---|
| Negative | Positive |
| | |

| Grandparenting | |
|---|---|
| Negative | Positive |
| | |

| Retirement | |
|---|---|
| Negative | Positive |
| | |

# Stages of Dying and Grieving

**Activity C**

**Chapter 21**

Name _____

Date _____ Period _____

The stages in the acceptance of death for the patient and the survivor are similar. In the spaces below, identify the five stages of dying and grieving. Next, in the first column, give an example of a typical behavior, statement, or feeling a patient might have during each of the stages of dying. In the second column, give an example of a typical behavior, statement, or feeling a survivor might have during the stages of grieving following the death of a loved one.

| Stages of Dying | Stages of Grieving |
|---|---|
| Stage one:_____ | |
| Stage two:_____ | |
| Stage three:_____ | |
| Stage four:_____ | |
| Stage five:_____ | |

# Terms Related to Death and Dying

**Activity D**

**Chapter 21**

Name _____

Date _____ Period _____

Match the following terms and identifying phrases.

_____ 1. A will that is oral.

_____ 2. Detailed physical examination of a dead body.

_____ 3. Person named in a will to receive the property of the dead person.

_____ 4. Will written in the handwriting of the person making the will.

_____ 5. Man whose wife has died.

_____ 6. Watch held over the body of a dead person before burial.

_____ 7. Legal document that allows people to choose whether or not they would be kept alive when there is apparently no hope for them to recover.

_____ 8. Woman whose husband has died.

_____ 9. Ceremony that causes people to confront the reality of death and helps them prepare to say a final good-bye to the dead person.

_____ 10. Some people make plans so when they die, all or parts of their bodies will be placed here until a need arises.

_____ 11. Persons who sign a will (in addition to the person for whom the will is written).

_____ 12. Dying without a will.

_____ 13. Medical facility designed for people who have only a short time to live.

_____ 14. Procedure in which the body of the deceased is reduced to ashes by burning.

A.  autopsy

B.  beneficiary

C.  cremated

D.  funeral

E.  holographic

F.  hospice

G.  intestate

H.  living will

I.  nuncupative

J.  organ bank

K.  wake

L.  widow

M.  widower

N.  witnesses

# 22 Providing for the Family's Physical Needs

## Consumer Terms

Name _____

Date _____ Period _____

Match the following terms and identifying phrases.

_____ 1. Anyone who buys goods and services.

_____ 2. Designed to get you into the store by offering an item at a low price.

_____ 3. Exaggerated claim used in advertising to attract the consumer.

_____ 4. Stimulates sales of goods and services by giving consumers information to influence their behavior.

_____ 5. In-depth studies done by advertisers to find out the psychological reasons people buy certain products.

_____ 6. False statement made to sound as if it were true.

_____ 7. Buying something that you had not planned to buy.

_____ 8. A public call for the return of a defective product.

_____ 9. Looking at different brands of the same or similar products within a store or among several stores.

_____ 10. The largest motivating reason for buying.

A. advertising

B. bait-and-switch

C. comparison shopping

D. consumer

E. habit

F. impulse buying

G. motivational research

H. recall

I. pseudo-truth

J. puffery

# Product Survey

**Activity B**                          Name _____

**Chapter 22**                        Date _____ Period _____

Group Members _____

_____

Work in a small group and select a product found in supermarkets, such as paper towels, coffee, peaches, or milk. Go to a store and survey every available variation of that product (for example, fresh, frozen, canned, or dehydrated). Record the information in the chart below. Complete the summary evaluation and report conclusions to the class.

Product evaluated _____

Store _____ Type of store (individually owned, national chain, etc.)_____

| Brand | Price | Package Size | Unit Price | Grade | Comments* |
|-------|-------|--------------|------------|-------|-----------|
|       |       |              |            |       |           |
|       |       |              |            |       |           |
|       |       |              |            |       |           |
|       |       |              |            |       |           |
|       |       |              |            |       |           |
|       |       |              |            |       |           |
|       |       |              |            |       |           |

*In the "Comments" column, list anything unique about the product. Do the labels make any special claims? Is the label particularly attractive or informative? Is the product tied in with a special promotion in any way?

**Summary Evaluation**

Best buy per unit _____

Best information on product_____

Best buy for single person_____

Best buy for married couple _____

Best buy for family of four _____

# Nutrition Label Analysis

**Activity C**

**Chapter 22**

Name _____

Date _____ Period _____

Imagine you are in the supermarket trying to decide between three kinds of breakfast cereal. You wish to buy the cereal that provides the highest nutritional value, the fewest calories, and the least fat. To help you analyze the cereals, consult the nutrition label on each and answer the questions below.

## Nutrition Labels

| **Nutrition Facts** | | |
|---|---|---|
| Serving Size      1 Cup (30g/1.1 oz.) | | |
| Servings Per Container                11 | | |
| **Amount Per Serving** | | **Cereal** |
| **Calories** | | **110** |
| Fat Calories | | 0 |
| | | **% Daily Value** |
| **Total Fat** 0g | | **0%** |
| Saturated Fat 0g | | **0%** |
| *Trans* Fat 0g | | |
| **Cholesterol** 0mg | | **0%** |
| **Sodium** 330mg | | **14%** |
| **Potassium** 35mg | | **1%** |
| **Total Carbohydrate** 26mg | | **9%** |
| Dietary Fiber 1g | | **4%** |
| Sugars 2g | | |
| Other Carbohydrates 23g | | |
| **Protein** 2g | | |

| **Nutrition Facts** | | |
|---|---|---|
| Serving Size          1 Cup (49g) | | |
| Servings Per Container   about 10 | | |
| **Amount Per Serving** | | **Cereal** |
| **Calories** | | **170** |
| Calories from Fat | | 5 |
| | | **% Daily Value** |
| **Total Fat** 0.5g | | **1%** |
| Saturated Fat 0g | | **0%** |
| *Trans* Fat 0g | | |
| Polyunsaturated Fat 0g | | |
| Monounsaturated Fat 0g | | |
| **Cholesterol** 0mg | | **0%** |
| **Sodium** 0mg | | **0%** |
| **Potassium** 200mg | | **6%** |
| **Total Carbohydrate** 41g | | **14%** |
| Dietary Fiber 5g | | **21%** |
| Insoluble Fiber 5g | | |
| Sugars 0g | | |
| Other Carbohydrates 23g | | |
| **Protein** 5g | | |

| **Nutrition Facts** | | |
|---|---|---|
| Serving Size          1/2 Cup (51) | | |
| Servings Per Container   about 18 | | |
| **Amount Per Serving** | | **Cereal** |
| **Calories** | | **220** |
| Calories from Fat | | 70 |
| | | **% Daily Value** |
| **Total Fat** 8g | | **12%** |
| Saturated Fat 3.5g | | **16%** |
| *Trans* Fat 1g | | |
| Polyunsaturated Fat 1g | | |
| Monounsaturated Fat 3g | | |
| **Cholesterol** 0mg | | **0%** |
| **Sodium** 20mg | | **1%** |
| **Potassium** 250mg | | **7%** |
| **Total Carbohydrate** 41g | | **12%** |
| Other Carbohydrates 17g | | |
| Dietary Fiber 4g | | **14%** |
| Sugars 15g | | |
| **Protein** 5g | | |

|           **Cereal A**            |           **Cereal B**            |           **Cereal C**            |

1. What is the size of a serving for Cereal A? _____

   What is the size of a serving for Cereal B? _____

   What is the size of a serving for Cereal C? _____

2. Which cereal has the fewest calories per serving?_____

   Which cereal has the most calories per serving? _____

3. Which cereal has the least total fat per serving? _____

   Which cereal has the most total fat per serving? _____

4. Which cereals have the least saturated fat per serving? _____

   Which cereal has the most saturated fat per serving?_____

5. Which cereal has the most protein per serving? _____

   Which cereal has the least protein per serving?_____

*(Continued)*

**Activity C** *(Continued)*                                   **Name**_____

6.  Which cereal is the highest in dietary fiber?_____

    Which cereal is the lowest in dietary fiber? _____

7.  Which cereal is highest in sugars? _____

    Which cereal is lowest in sugars?_____

8.  Which cereal provides the highest percentage daily value of sodium? _____

9.  Which cereal do you consider the most healthful? State the reasons for your choice as well as any reservations you may have about your choice. _____

    _____

    _____

    _____

    _____

    _____

# Making Housing Decisions

**Activity D**

**Chapter 22**

Name _____

Date _____ Period _____

Working with a classmate, locate a rental property to visit in your community. Obtain a copy of the lease, if available. Answer the following questions concerning the property and rental arrangements. Be prepared to share this information with your class in order to determine the best rental properties available in your community.

1. Is the rental unit a house, apartment, or townhouse? _____

2. What is the address? _____

3. How did you find out about the property? _____

4. What is the monthly rent? _____

## Lease and Security Deposit

1. Is there a written lease? _____

2. For what length of time is the lease written? _____

3. Is the tenant responsible for such expenses as water, electricity, gas, lawn care, and repairs? _____

_____

If so, list the items and the anticipated monthly amounts.

_____

_____

_____

4. Does the lease have an automatic renewal clause that requires ample notification if a tenant plans to move? _____

_____

5. Does the lease prevent the tenant from allowing someone else to move in with them? _____

6. Are there any restrictions in the lease concerning children, pets, etc.? _____

If so, explain what they are. _____

7. Does the lease restrict assigning or subletting? _____

8. What is the amount of the security deposit, if any? _____

9. Do the tenants receive back the entire security deposit when they move? _____

10. Are there extra charges for additional services? _____

If so, list the charges. _____

_____

*(Continued)*

**Activity D** (*Continued*)      Name _____

# Dwelling Checklist

| Yes | No | |
|-----|-----|---|
| _____ | _____ | 1. Is the dwelling close to public transportation? |
| _____ | _____ | 2. Is there laundry equipment in the unit or house? |
| _____ | _____ | 3. Is the laundry room easily accessible, safe, and available at reasonable hours? |
| _____ | _____ | 4. Are the provisions for mail and parcel delivery adequate? |
| _____ | _____ | 5. Are there adequate security provisions? |
| _____ | _____ | 6. Are the halls, stairwells, and elevators well-lighted? |
| _____ | _____ | 7. Are there safe fire exits and smoke detectors? |
| _____ | _____ | 8. Are the garbage disposal facilities adequate and convenient? |
| _____ | _____ | 9. Is there a resident manager or superintendent? |
| _____ | _____ | 10. Is there a swimming pool? |
| _____ | _____ | 11. Is there a recreation facility for large groups? |

# Unit Checklist

| Yes | No | |
|-----|-----|---|
| _____ | _____ | 1. Is the unit furnished? |
| _____ | _____ | 2. Is carpeting included, and is it clean and in good condition? |
| _____ | _____ | 3. Are walls clean and in good condition? |
| _____ | _____ | 4. Can windows be opened and are they clean? |
| _____ | _____ | 5. Are there screens on the windows and are they in good condition? |
| _____ | _____ | 6. Will the outside of the windows be cleaned by building maintenance? |
| _____ | _____ | 7. Is there air conditioning? |
| _____ | _____ | 8. Is heating adequate with controls in each unit? |
| _____ | _____ | 9. Are window treatments included, and are they clean and in good condition? |
| _____ | _____ | 10. Are there sufficient electrical wall outlets? |
| _____ | _____ | 11. Do light switches control wall outlets? |
| _____ | _____ | 12. Is there a deck or patio area? |
| _____ | _____ | 13. Is management responsible for outside maintenance? |
| _____ | _____ | 14. Are bathroom facilities clean and in good working condition? |
| _____ | _____ | 15. Is the hot water supply adequate? |
| _____ | _____ | 16. Will the unit be freshly painted for new tenants? |
| _____ | _____ | 17. Does management pay for any redecorating the tenants may choose to do? |
| _____ | _____ | 18. Is there adequate closet space? |
| _____ | _____ | 19. Do outside doors have dead bolt locks and see-through viewers? |
| _____ | _____ | 20. Is the kitchen clean and in good working condition? |
| _____ | _____ | 21. Is there adequate cupboard space? |
| _____ | _____ | 22. Is there a dishwasher? |
| _____ | _____ | 23. Are there extra features in the kitchen? |
| _____ | _____ | 24. Are there any "house rules," such as no loud music or TV after certain hours, that are unacceptable |

# 23 Protecting the Family's Resources

## Insurance Opinions

Activity A

Chapter 23

Name _____

Date _____ Period _____

Read the following statements concerning insurance. Place a check in the column that best describes your opinion. Discuss the statements in class.

**Agree  Disagree  Unsure**

_____  _____  _____  1. There is no such thing as being overinsured.

_____  _____  _____  2. It can be risky to admit wrongdoing at the scene of an auto accident.

_____  _____  _____  3. Having a comprehensive program of insurance coverage contributes to a person's peace of mind.

_____  _____  _____  4. Paying life insurance premiums amounts to nothing more than paying a company who is betting you will die at a certain age.

_____  _____  _____  5. It is illegal and unethical to commit insurance fraud.

_____  _____  _____  6. Paying health insurance premiums is a waste of money when a person is young and healthy.

_____  _____  _____  7. Every member of a young family needs life insurance.

_____  _____  _____  8. If you are involved in a major car accident, you should call your insurance agent immediately after calling the ambulance and the police so the agent can visit the accident site if necessary.

_____  _____  _____  9. It is better not to report minor accidents to your insurance company so your insurance rates do not go up.

_____  _____  _____  10. Renters do not need personal property insurance.

Select a statement from above.

I strongly agree with statement _____ because _____

_____

_____

_____

I strongly disagree with statement _____ because _____

_____

_____

_____

# Insurance Terms

Activity B

Chapter 23

Name _____

Date _____ Period _____

_____  1.  The legal contract issued by an insurance company.

_____  2.  Property _____ liability insurance pays for legal defense and the damage your car causes to the property of others.

_____  3.  Type of life insurance that offers both protection and savings. Part of the premium goes into savings invested in equity products.

_____  4.  A(n) _____ clause states the policyholder will pay a certain percentage of the costs, perhaps 20 to 25 percent, and the insurance company will pay the remaining portion of the costs.

_____  5.  _____ life insurance is designed to cover a person's entire life and to build up cash values.

_____  6.  _____ insurance protects you against financial loss when your car is damaged by something other than another vehicle, such as fire, theft, hail, or vandalism.

_____  7.  A(n) _____ clause states the insured will pay an agreed-on portion of the total expense, such as $250, and the insurance company will pay the balance of the bill.

_____  8.  Type of life insurance that covers the policyholder for a specified period of time and builds no cash value.

_____  9.  Type of car insurance that, in theory, eliminates the legal process of proving who caused an accident.

_____  10. Amount of money a policyholder pays for an insurance policy.

_____  11. The _____ amount of a life insurance policy indicates the total amount of money to be paid upon the death of the policyholder.

_____  12. Person designated by a life insurance policyholder to receive the benefits of the policy upon the policyholder's death.

_____  13. _____ insurance protects you against financial loss when your car is damaged by another vehicle or object or as a result of turning over the car.

_____  14. Bodily _____ liability insurance pays for damages and legal defense if you hurt others while driving.

# Insurance Decisions

**Activity C**

**Chapter 23**

Name _____

Date _____ Period _____

In a small group, discuss the following situations. Then write down your group's conclusions and be prepared to share them with the whole class.

Group members:_____

**Situation A:**

Amarika is a healthy young single woman who has just started her first full-time job. She must decide which type of health insurance she wants: the low-option (pays for fewer kinds of illness/surgery, with a higher deductible and lower premiums), or the high-option (pays for more kinds of illness/surgery, with a lower deductible and higher premiums). She has sought the advice of her uncle, who says she should get the high-option plan because "When it comes to insurance, you can't win—but you sure can lose." What does her uncle mean by his statement? Which type of insurance would you advise Amarika to get? Why?

_____

_____

_____

_____

_____

_____

_____

_____

_____

_____

**Situation B:**

John, a young clergyperson, was involved in a major car accident late one night as he was driving home from a church meeting. Both drivers were equally at fault. Conscience-stricken, John admitted his driving mistakes immediately and begged the forgiveness of the other driver. Now the other driver is suing John for a large sum of money, using John's "confession" against him. John's insurance agent says you should never discuss fault at the scene of an accident without your lawyer present. Is John's insurance agent correct? Why? What should John have done if he had mixed feelings about his driving mistake?

_____

_____

_____

_____

_____

_____

_____

_____

_____

*(Continued)*

**Activity C** *(Continued)*                          **Name** _____

### Situation C:

Mildred lives in a home that has two steps in front without a railing. Last January, her elderly friend Victoria came over for afternoon coffee. The steps were icy. As Victoria was leaving, Mildred said, "Do you need some help getting down the steps?" Victoria replied, "No, I think I can make it." Then she slipped and fractured her hip in two places. Mildred was shocked when she received notification that Victoria was suing her for negligence in not having the steps free of ice. Who is in the right? What could Mildred have done to avoid this situation?

_____

_____

_____

_____

_____

_____

_____

### Situation D:

Your classmate Will say that while he was waiting at a stoplight recently, his car's back bumper was tapped gently from behind by another car. Will has heard that you can get whiplash from collisions. Though he feels fine, he says he is tempted to fake a whiplash injury in order to try to collect an insurance settlement. What would you tell Will?

_____

_____

_____

_____

_____

_____

_____

### Situation E:

Lisa and Rajani own a small condo with a washer-dryer combination appliance they bought and had installed. Because they are just starting out and do not have much furniture, they decided against getting personal property insurance. Last night, after Lisa and Rajani returned home from work, they received a call from the neighbor in the condo below them. A hose in their washer/dryer had slipped and had caused $5,000 of water damage to the apartment below. What should Lisa and Rajani do now? Should they have obtained personal property insurance when they first bought the condo?

_____

_____

_____

_____

_____

_____

_____

# 24 Using Banking Services

## Survey of Financial Institutions

**Activity A**

**Chapter 24**

Name _____

Date _____ Period _____

Survey two financial institutions in your area regarding services they offer. Try to include two different types of financial institutions (commercial banks, savings banks, credit unions, etc.). Report your findings to the class and share any literature provided by the institution.

Financial institution name: _____

Type of financial institution: _____

This financial institution is insured by: _____

Types of accounts available and brief description of accounts (including interest rates):

_____

_____

_____

_____

_____

Financial institution name: _____

Type of financial institution: _____

This financial institution is insured by: _____

Types of accounts available and brief description of accounts (including interest rates):

_____

_____

_____

_____

_____

If you were opening a checking account, which of these two financial institutions would you choose? Explain your answer.

_____

_____

# Writing Checks

**Activity B**                                         Name _____

**Chapter 24**                                        Date _____ Period _____

1. Make the check below payable for $75 to Carmen L. Lopez, M.D., to pay her for an office visit. Be sure to observe the rules for correctly writing a check.

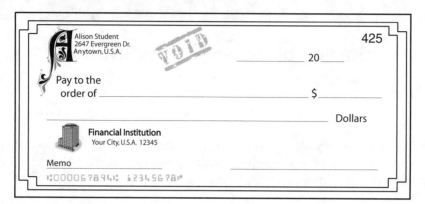

2. Make the check below payable to yourself for $100 so you can withdraw money from your checking account.

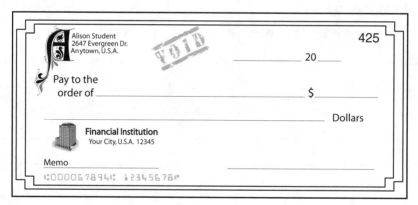

3. To endorse and deposit a check that has been made payable to you,

    A. what do you write on the back of the check? _____

    B. on which end of the check do you write the above information? _____

    _____

4. If you wish to endorse the check and then make it payable to Joe Kim, what do you write? _____

    _____

5. Name five rules for correctly writing a check.

    A. _____

    B. _____

    C. _____

    D. _____

    E. _____

# Monetary Pyramid

**Activity C**

**Chapter 24**

Name _____

Date _____ Period _____

Read the definitions and write the terms in the corresponding spaces on the pyramid.

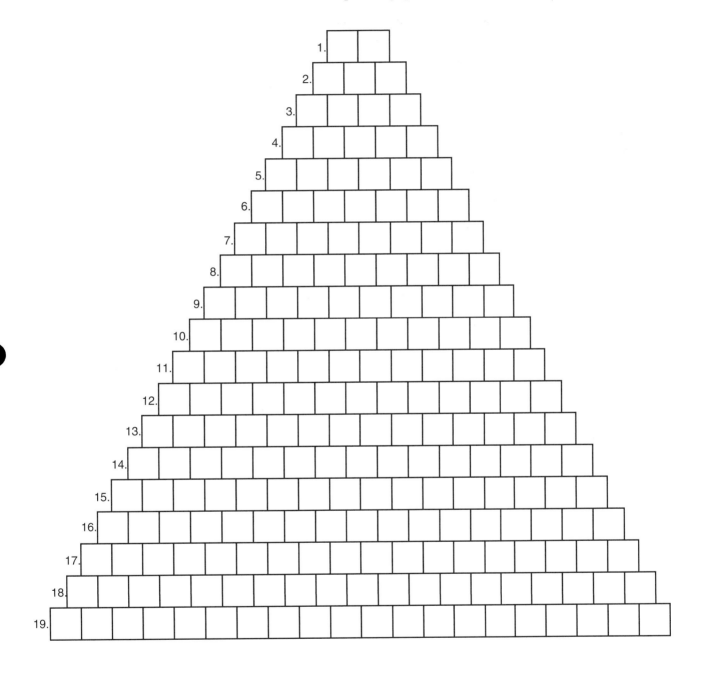

*(Continued)*

**Activity C** *(Continued)*                         **Name** _____

1. The form that allows an employer to determine how much of an employee's pay should be withheld for taxes.

2. The amount of money left in your paycheck after deductions have been taken out.

3. The abbreviation for the act under which you pay Social Security taxes.

4. The income you receive before deductions are taken from your pay.

5. A type of check deposit service in which the employer's payroll monies are electronically transferred into their employees' personal checking or savings accounts.

6. A type of account that can be opened with a small amount of money and allows you to make deposits and withdrawals. It pays a low rate of interest.

7. A return on an investment paid according to a specified annual percentage of the amount of money in an account.

8. Occurs when a check is written on an account with insufficient funds.

9. Sources or amounts of income that are not taxed.

10. The income you accumulate before deductions are made. (two words)

11. A form of savings offered by the U.S. government, issued in specific denominations. (two words)

12. Vacation pay, sick leave, retirement funds, and insurance provided by employers. (two words)

13. Taxes collected to provide disability, survivors, and retirement benefits when needed. (two words)

14. The money your employer withholds for federal income tax purposes is sent to the _____ _____ service.

15. Allows both the husband and wife to deposit and withdraw money from the same place. (three words)

16. A long-range savings plan designed to provide income after you stop working. (two words)

17. A convenient type of investment for savings where the interest rate changes daily. (three words)

18. Form W-2, which your employer sends to you for use in filling out your income tax return. (four words)

19. A form of investment that requires you to commit a minimum amount of money for a set period of time. (three words)

# Financial Decisions

**Activity D**

**Chapter 24**

Name_____

Date_____ Period_____

In a small group, discuss the following situations. Then write down your group's conclusions and be prepared to present them to the whole class.

Group members:_____

**Situation A:**

Joni and Jack, a dual-career, two-car couple, started out in their marriage making similar salaries. Each had a checking account, and major expenses such as rent, groceries, and vacations were split 50-50. Any remaining funds were saved or spent on clothes, recreation, etc. Lately, Joni's career has taken off, and she has received some big raises and bonuses. She is spending a lot on clothes, recreation, antiques, and works of original art for the apartment. She is also about to buy an expensive sports car to drive to work. Although he is proud of her, Jack is beginning to feel like Joni's "poor" husband.

Jack's parents say a 50-50 split on expenses is unfair when one spouse makes a much higher salary than the other. They say expenses should be allocated proportionately to the salaries. For example, the spouse who makes only ⅓ as much as the other should pay only ⅓ of the expenses. Do you agree with this? Why? Are there any other solutions the couple could try?

_____
_____
_____
_____
_____

**Situation B:**

Allen, a 24-year-old single person, is evaluating two job offers. The jobs have roughly equivalent responsibilities and excellent prospects for advancement. However, the benefits and salaries differ. Job A offers a moderate salary and the following benefits: a pension plan with generous employer contributions; a range of first-rate health insurance plans; employer-paid life insurance with a face value of $150,000; and 20 days of paid vacation leave per year. In contrast, Job B offers a yearly salary that is $5,000 higher than Job A, no pension plan, no life insurance, one HMO health insurance plan, and 10 days of paid vacation leave per year. Which job do you think Allen should take, and why?

_____
_____
_____
_____
_____

*(Continued)*

**Activity D** *(Continued)*                           Name_____

### Situation C:

Julie and Chuck have three children, ages 1, 3, and 4. Chuck works full-time as a social worker, but the couple are having trouble making ends meet financially. Julie has been looking for a job and is evaluating two offers. Job A is her "dream job"—a boss she likes and who is willing to train her; interesting, challenging work; and excellent chances for advancement. However, most of her earnings will be offset by the cost of hiring someone to take care of the children. Job B is okay, though it has none of the advantages of Job A. However, it has an excellent on-site child care facility that is mostly paid for by the company. Which job would you choose if you were Julie, and why?

_____

_____

_____

_____

_____

### Situation D:

Amy and Eddie have just moved to the area and are trying to decide which bank to use. Eddie wants to use Bank A because it has a branch office near his office and offers check overdraft protection and home equity loans. Amy wants to bank with the credit union at her workplace because the credit union offers convenience, a wide range of services, and low-interest loans. Which bank should they choose? Do Amy and Eddie have to bank at the same financial institution? Why or why not?

_____

_____

_____

_____

_____

# 25 Managing Your Finances

## How Well Do You Manage Money?

Activity A

Chapter 25

Name _____

Date _____ Period _____

Evaluate your money management practices by answering the questions below. Then total the number of "yes" responses you checked and learn how well you manage your money.

| Yes | No | | |
|-----|-----|-----|---|
| _____ | _____ | 1. | Do you currently have a personal budget or spending plan? |
| _____ | _____ | 2. | Do you keep a record of the money you spend? |
| _____ | _____ | 3. | Do you and your family plan together the use of family funds? |
| _____ | _____ | 4. | If your grandparents gave you $75, would you be able to save it for a future goal? |
| _____ | _____ | 5. | Do you have your own checking account? |
| _____ | _____ | 6. | Do you have your own savings account? |
| _____ | _____ | 7. | Have you ever been able to save $100 or more for a specific goal within a year's time or less? |
| _____ | _____ | 8. | Would you ask to have money deducted from your paycheck and put into a savings plan if it were available where you worked? |
| _____ | _____ | 9. | Would you postpone a vacation if you had to pay for it on credit? |
| _____ | _____ | 10. | Do you know how you spent your last $20? |
| _____ | _____ | 11. | Do you always pay back money you borrow from your friends or family? |
| _____ | _____ | 12. | Do you have money set aside for unexpected needs? |
| _____ | _____ | 13. | Do you plan your shopping trips and buy just what you have on your list? |
| _____ | _____ | 14. | If you need to make a major purchase, do you shop around for the best price and quality? |
| _____ | _____ | 15. | If you know of a future need for money, such as for college tuition or a major purchase, do you make a plan for meeting that financial goal? |
| _____ | _____ | 16. | Are you able to avoid impulse buying when you do not really need the item that is such a bargain? |
| _____ | _____ | 17. | Do you read the labels and instructions that are included with items you purchase? |
| _____ | _____ | 18. | Do you carefully evaluate the cost of using credit rather than automatically charging everything you purchase? |
| _____ | _____ | 19. | Are you able to avoid continually asking others for money? |
| _____ | _____ | 20. | Do you know how much money you have with you now without looking? |

*(Continued)*

**Activity A** (*Continued*)          **Name** _____

Total number of "yes" responses: _____

If you answered "yes" to 15 or more questions, you have developed excellent skills in managing your finances.
If you answered "yes" to at least 10 questions, you are on your way to becoming a good money manager.
If you answered "yes" to less than 10 questions, you may need to work on your money management skills.
Review the questions to which you answered "no." How can you improve your money management skills?

_____

_____

_____

_____

_____

_____

_____

_____

_____

_____

_____

# Saving vs. Spending

**Activity B**

**Chapter 25**

Name _____

Date _____ Period _____

Respond to each of the following statements. Then describe the saving system you plan to follow if you get married.

**Agree  Disagree  Unsure**

_____ _____ _____ 1. I believe a couple should save as much money as they spend on recreation.

_____ _____ _____ 2. I believe a young couple have plenty of time to save money and they should enjoy their youth and not worry about saving money.

_____ _____ _____ 3. I believe a young couple should start to save as much as possible in order to purchase their first home as quickly as possible.

_____ _____ _____ 4. If one spouse believes in saving money and the other sees no need to save money, their marriage could have some serious problems.

_____ _____ _____ 5. In order to save money, you have to become a penny-pincher and deprive yourself and your spouse of wanted items.

_____ _____ _____ 6. A good way to save money is to deposit a certain percentage of every paycheck in your savings account before any money is spent.

_____ _____ _____ 7. Saving in a piggy bank is smart because the money is available quickly for emergencies.

_____ _____ _____ 8. If both spouses work, they should each put the same amount into savings each month.

_____ _____ _____ 9. In a dual-worker family, couples can save money fairly quickly if they can live on one income and save the other.

_____ _____ _____ 10. Couples on a budget should allot a small amount of money each month for each spouse to spend as he or she wishes.

Describe the saving system you plan to follow if you get married. _____

_____

_____

_____

_____

_____

_____

# Budget for a Young Married Couple

**Activity C**

**Chapter 25**

Name _____

Date _____ Period _____

Val and Joe were married last summer shortly after they graduated from high school. They have prepared a budget, but are having trouble saving money for future goals. They would like to take a vacation next summer to celebrate their first wedding anniversary. The travel agent has told them about a 4-day trip to Orlando that includes hotel and airfare for $900 from Chicago. They would like to take an additional $700 for meals and entertainment expenses.

The total they would need for the trip is $1600. Their anniversary is six months away.

Using the figures below, fill in the monthly budget form on the opposite page. List first the budget amounts that Val and Joe decided upon in the column marked "Planned." Then list the actual expenses they incurred this month in the column marked "Actual." Decide whether each item is a fixed expense (those that are a specific amount each month) or a flexible expense (those that vary in amount each month). List each item in the appropriate place on the budget form. Val and Joe's combined net monthly income is $2400.

Val and Joe's budget includes the following items:

| | | | |
|---|---|---|---|
| rent | $600 | personal care | $120 |
| electricity | 40 | gas and oil | 95 |
| car payment | 300 | medical care | 35 |
| telephone | 55 | entertainment | 300 |
| train fare | 95 | and leisure | |
| car insurance | 90 | clothing | 180 |
| life insurance | 25 | gifts and | 110 |
| food | 355 | contributions | |

Val and Joe's actual expenses for this month were:

| | | | |
|---|---|---|---|
| rent | $600 | personal care | $129 |
| electricity | 33 | gas and oil | 115 |
| car payment | 300 | medical care | 72 |
| telephone | 62 | entertainment | 228 |
| train fare | 90 | and leisure | |
| car insurance | 90 | clothing | 266 |
| life insurance | 25 | gifts and | 78 |
| food | 339 | contributions | |

*(Continued)*

**Activity C** *(Continued)*　　　　　　　　Name _____

## Monthly Budget

| Monthly net income: | | | | |
|---|---|---|---|---|
| **Fixed expenses:** | **Planned** | **Actual** | **Amount Over/Under** | **Revised Budget** |
| | | | | |
| | | | | |
| | | | | |
| | | | | |
| | | | | |
| | | | | |
| **Flexible expenses:** | | | | |
| | | | | |
| | | | | |
| | | | | |
| | | | | |
| | | | | |
| | | | | |
| | | | | |
| | | | | |
| | | | | |
| | | | | |
| | | | | |
| | | | | |
| | | | | |
| | | | | |
| **Savings** | | | | |
| **Totals** | | | | |

After all items have been listed, total both columns to see whether Val and Joe went over or were under their budget for the month. Then in the column marked "Amount Over/Under," determine how much they went over or under their budget in each expense category. If they went over the budgeted amount, precede the amount with a + sign. If they spent less than the budgeted amount, precede the amount with a – sign. Answer the following questions.

*(Continued)*

**Activity C** (*Continued*)                                   **Name** _____

1. How much money will Val and Joe have to save each month in order to go to Orlando on their anniversary? _____

2. How would you revise Val and Joe's budget in order for them to make the trip? Write your revised budget in the last column on the budget form. _____

_____

_____

3. Which items will you have Val and Joe cut back on in your revised budget? List each item you have cut and explain your decision. _____

_____

_____

_____

4. Are there any items in their budget that you revised upwards? If so, list and explain below.

_____

_____

_____

5. Describe two other options Val and Joe could consider if they did not want to save for this vacation six months from now.

Option one: _____

_____

_____

Option two: _____

_____

_____

6. Val and Joe would like to buy a second car so they do not have to pay $90 each month for train fare for Val to go to work. Considering their budget items, what would be your advice to them?

_____

_____

_____

7. Val and Joe hope to start a family soon. How will this decision affect their budget? _____

_____

_____

_____

_____

8. It is a good idea to put at least 10% of your net income into savings each month for unexpected expenses. Val and Joe's original budget does not include savings. What categories would you change in their original budget so they could save $240 a month? List and explain the changes you would make. _____

_____

_____

_____

_____

# Love and Money

**Activity D**

**Chapter 25**

Name _____

Date _____ Period _____

In a small group, discuss the following situations. Then write your conclusions and be prepared to share them with the whole class.

Group members:_____

**Situation A:**
Though they have a credit card, Ed and Cora believe long-term credit use is a very poor practice because of the interest charges. This month, they have had heavy car repair expenses that have used up their savings. Now their 15-year-old daughter, Gabrielle, has a deep cavity in her tooth. The dentist says she will lose the tooth if it is not fixed very soon. The dentist is willing to accept a credit card as payment. How can Gabrielle convince her parents to use their credit card to pay the dentist?

_____

_____

_____

_____

_____

**Situation B:**
Tyreese and Rayetta are a young couple who love each other but who are having a difficult time adjusting to married life. Tyreese can be insensitive, and Rayetta can be overly sensitive. Every time they have a disagreement, Tyreese goes out and uses his credit card to charge perfume, clothing, and jewelry. Then he brings the gifts to Rayetta as a way of saying "I'm sorry." Rayetta is getting very uneasy as their credit balances are adding up. What should she say to Tyreese?

_____

_____

_____

_____

_____

**Situation C:**
Chrissie and Noah have just married. Noah has several credit cards in his name. Chrissie has none. The couple have decided that Chrissie will work outside the home only until she becomes pregnant. After that, she plans to be a full-time homemaker for the indefinite future. Chrissie's older sister Paula says that while Chrissie is working and has an income, she ought to apply for a credit card in her own name because it may be difficult to get one later. Chrissie feels she will never need a credit card or credit history of her own because her marriage will be perfect. What would you advise Chrissie?

_____

_____

_____

_____

*(Continued)*

**Activity D** *(Continued)*                                           **Name** _____

### Situation D:

Koshiro and Nalani are having trouble sticking to their budget. Koshiro has a college education, and Nalani does not. Every time Nalani misuses or mispronounces a word in front of their friends, Koshiro is embarrassed and corrects her. To get even, Nalani takes the credit card and goes out on a buying spree. It takes months for the couple to get their budget back on track after one of these sprees. Koshiro is discouraged and wonders if there's any use trying to budget. How would you advise the couple?

_____

_____

_____

_____

_____

### Situation E:

Andrew and Ava have a basically good marriage. They both believe in saving money, but Ava, who was raised in a poor family, has especially strong views. As the financial manager of the household, she insists that Andrew account for every penny he spends. If he brings home a purchase Ava disapproves of, she criticizes him sharply and nags him until he returns the item. He says nothing because he was taught as a boy that it is wrong to "answer back" to a wife or mother. Lately, Andrew finds that he is avoiding going home. He either goes out with his friends or works late with his young unmarried coworker, who seems to accept and understand him. Should Andrew try to talk to Ava? What should he say?

_____

_____

_____

_____

_____

_____

_____